# ALLYSON COOPER

# Cricut Project Ideas

Your Special Guide To Start Creating Your Projects, With Different Ideas From Beginners to Expert

Copyright © 2020 Allyson Cooper

All rights reserved

© **Copyright 2020 - All rights reserved.**

The content contained within this book may not be reproduced, duplicated or transmitted without direct written permission from the author or the publisher.

Under no circumstances will any blame or legal responsibility be held against the publisher, or author, for any damages, reparation, or monetary loss due to the information contained within this book. Either directly or indirectly.

**Legal Notice:**

This book is copyright protected. This book is only for personal use. You cannot amend, distribute, sell, use, quote or paraphrase any part, or the content within this book, without the consent of the author or publisher.

**Disclaimer Notice:**

Please note the information contained within this document is for educational and entertainment purposes only. All effort has been executed to present accurate, up to date, and reliable, complete information. No warranties of any kind are declared or implied. Readers acknowledge that the author is not engaging in the rendering of legal, financial, medical or professional advice. The content within this book has been derived from various sources. Please consult a licensed professional before attempting any techniques outlined in this book.

By reading this document, the reader agrees that under no circumstances is the author responsible for any losses, direct or indirect, which are incurred as a result of the use of information contained within this document, including, but not limited to, — errors, omissions, or inaccuracies.

# CRICUT FOR BEGINNERS

*Introduction* ............................................................................... *5*

*Chapter 1. Cricut Design Space Project Ideas* ................................ *10*

*Chapter 2. List Of Materials That Can Be Used With Compatible Cricut Machines* ........................................................................... *17*

*Chapter 3. Materials For Cricut Machines* ................................... *26*

*Chapter 4. Easy Cricut Project Ideas* ............................................ *34*

*Chapter 5. Paper-Based Projects* ................................................... *43*

*Chapter 6. Cricut Projects With Vinyl* .......................................... *52*

*Chapter 7. Project To Create Fabric Cuts (Part 1)* ......................... *62*

*Chapter 8. Project To Create Fabric Cuts (Part 2)* ......................... *79*

*Chapter 9. Project With Glass* ..................................................... *88*

*Chapter 10. Other Ideas For Advanced Level* ................................ *95*

*Chapter 11. Other Projects Using Cricut Design Space* ................ *104*

*Chapter 12. Other Projects Using Cricut Design Spacc (Part 2)* .. *115*

*Conclusion* ............................................................................... *139*

# Introduction

A Cricut machine permits us to do projects with insane exactness since it replaces what we would routinely cut with either scissors or an x-acto. Including inconspicuous speed and quality. You can get to their library of the plan by subscription by paying per project OR (and this is the thing that I like the most) you can transfer your records and work of art! This little force wonder permits creatives a smooth, experience as we've never had before. With the Cricut machines, you can make not just paper crafts or modifying clothing with vinyl, carving, or stenciling. In any case, cut texture and more than 100 different materials. The people at Cricut are additionally altering the business by carrying sublimation printing to crafter's fingertips with perhaps the most recent discharge, Infusible Ink! The introduction of Infusible Ink items have been a distinct advantage because Infusible Ink heat moves are always implanted into your base material. They keep going as long as the undertaking itself. No chipping, no stripping, no splitting, and no wrinkling—ever! So, to summarize, a Cricut machine is your envisioned right hand with regards to making!

Cricut Design Space is a web-based program just as a partner application and now a beta Desktop software that permits you to make, transfer, and oversee records to work the Cricut Maker and Cricut Explore machines. You can get to the application remotely in individual machines, utilizing your PC, tablet, and even your cell phone. Cricut Design Space™ additionally permits you to get to a library of tasks and files to download.

Imagine if Pinterest had a baby with an otherworldly site that fundamentally does all your creating for you. That is the Cricut Design Space. Cricut Design Space is a web-based program that lets you peruse pages and pages of predesigned extensions to structure your projects on your work area, computer, tablet, and phone. Cricut Design Space houses more than 75,000 pictures, 400 fonts, and more than 800 predesigned Make It Now projects. The Make It Now areas are far accomplished for you, and all you need to do is to click "Go."

Cricut Design Space additionally lets you transfer your JPEG and SVG files just as your fonts. It's a workhorse. Talk has it the Design Space can likewise foresee the winning lottery numbers for the following ten years. That is false.

What Is Cricut Access?

If you somehow happened to mosey on over to Cricut Design Space right this second... proceed... I'll pause.

Did you mosey?

Presently, without a Design Space Subscription, you'll pay about a buck for each picture you use, and about $3-7 for each Make It Now venture you buy. It'll fundamentally work as an "individual" administration. You'll pick what you need, and you'll pay for it. I loathe that thought. I detest paying for things.

Cricut Access is the service for all you folks who likewise prefer not to pay for things. Cricut Access gives you access to a vast number of pictures, text styles, full cartridges, and Make It Now extensions at no extra expense. Here is how it works:

**What Do I Get?**

Well—it'll rely upon which Cricut Access participation you pick—don't stress—they're all extraordinary.

Monthly:

- Pay $9.99 on a month-to-month premise and get boundless access to more than 400 fonts and 75,000 pictures... no compelling reason to follow through on individual costs for every textual style you love.
- 10% off of all requests on the Cricut website and 10% off of licensed images.
- The simplicity of scanning for Cricut Access pictures because of the convenient minimal green flags that direct you to all photographs, cartridges, textual styles, and activities that are saved for your account.

*Yearly:*

Just like the month to month subscription. When you pay for an entire year, you save money!

***Premium:***

Identical benefits as the month-to-month and yearly subscriptions, with that special reward of more reserve funds like FREE transporting on orders over $50!

**What Don't I Get?**

There are a few pictures, fonts, and activities that won't be remembered for your Cricut Access membership, however, you do get 10% off any Design Space content that you'd need to pay for out of pocket

Cricut Access membership doesn't permit you to utilize your 10% markdown on the renewal of your Cricut Access memberships... shucks.

**How Much Does It Cost?**

Now, how about we talk dollar bills! There are two options:

- You can pay for the entire year without a moment's delay for $95.80, which comes to about $7.99 per month OR
- You can pay $9.99 per month for your membership with the alternative to drop whenever.

Whichever way you go, you'll have boundless access to a vast amount of substance and all that could be needed to start creating. I like to take the "pull out all the stops" alternative and pay for everything in advance. That way, come June, I've disregarded that $95.80, and I incline that I am merely getting everything for free!!!! (I know everyone will be with me on this).

## For What Reason Should I Care?

Here is how I see it: if you possess a Cricut Explore Air or Cricut Maker, at that point, Cricut Access is the best way to go. You burned through all that cash on a great machine so you would do well to utilize it. Try not to let it sit in the corner and transform into a brightening rack. Set that awful kid to work! It will astound you, and in a matter of hours, you'll be snared. With my Cricut Access participation, I concoct many reasons under the sun to utilize my machine. You'll discover pictures that you never knew existed, and you'll have a fabulous time using them in imaginative manners.

Amazing—and remember, you'll get 10% off every one of those provisions from the Cricut website, which incorporates mats, cutting edges, vinyl, Easy Press machines, and tools among loads of different things.

# Chapter 1. Cricut Design Space Project Ideas

**Craft Ideas for Your Cricut Cutting Machine**

Want any Cricut ideas for the cutting software for your Cricut? Cricut personal electric cutters are revolutionizing handcrafts, and the amount of creative and beautiful things they can suddenly do are astounding people around the world.

The way a Cricut works is simple: just load one of the many cartridges available into the cutter, choose what color card stock you'd like to work with for that particular design, and cut away. Each cartridge has a number of thematic designs-anything from seasonal designs to favorite superheroes-and Cricut users can choose from each cartridge one or more designs. Then, the designs cut out are fixed on.

- Fitting the wall
- Scrapbooks
- Photo frames
- Custom greeting cards-you call them-as with a Cricut, anything is possible.

Maybe the most endearing idea for Cricut craft would be a Cricut calendar. With each month, a separate page might be created, and each of these separate pages could be decorated with different designs. July, for instance, will be trimmed with the designs used in the Seasonal Cartridge Independence Day, while February is the obvious choice for the Seasonal Cartridge Love Struck. However, the fun isn't stopping there, and the Mother's Day Cartridge would be perfect for May, while the Easter Cartridge is a natural April. Cricut-land is unique to December, and Cricut handlers have numerous sets of designs to choose from, like the Joys of the Season Cartridge besides the Snow Friends Cartridge.

What would life be without scrapbooks to document our most precious belongings of every single waking moment: our children? Scrapbooks can be customized to each and every child with the Cricut cutting machine, and what could be better than, for mother and daughter or father and son, to settle down together and choose with which images they wish to decorate their own pictures. Cricut also knows that boys and girls are different and that while the boys probably won't like using the Once Upon a Princess Cartridge, they'd definitely go wild over the Batman: The Brave and The Bold Cartridge. On the other hand, little girls would probably turn their dainty noses up at the Robotz Cartridge but love the Disney Tinker Bell and Friends Cartridge. For Cricut scrapbooking ideas, you never will be at a loss.

Nevertheless, your Cricut layout ideas are not only limited to photos, and there are also alphabets available-such as the Sesame Street Font Cartridge, and the Ashlyn's Alphabet Cartridge-that would be handy whenever it's time to customize a gift. Ideal gifts should include pictures of beloved pets-or even vinyl wall-hangings commemorating a special event such as that overseas trip-all embellished with beautiful and colorful Cricut cut-outs of course. Cricut provides for every possibility, and at this time they Create a Critter Cartridge and the Seasonal Cartridge Summer in Paris would be perfect to accompany your Cricut home decor. Birthdays, Christmas, Graduations, Bar Mitzvahs, baby showers: the list of presents is boundless, and that does not even comprise those ventures "made for fun." Cricut has cartridges that can be thought of to match every single occasion-and every single project. Completing a Cricut project together is also a great way for a family to bond with each other, and the beautiful things made together can be treasured for a lifetime. With a personal electric cutter from Cricut, only the sky and your imagination is the limit.

**Awesome Cricut Card Ideas for Your Family**

Now that you own a Cricut cutting tool, why waste another penny on a store-bought greeting card. For the Cricut, you charged a lot so let's put it to work. Here are just a couple of Cricut Card Ideas that will get you started and let you use some of your chosen Cricut cartridges. The next calendar holiday coming up is Easter.

I think of how your family and friends will react when they receive a handmade greeting card made by YOU when I think of what Cricut card ideas I can come up with. Now that you've got your Cricut cutting machine, and a variety of Cricut cartridges, adding your personal touch to a card is so easy.

If the Cricut Doodle charms cartridge is one of the Cricut cartridges you have, you can make a really cute handmade Easter Bunny greeting card or an Easter Basket filled with colored eggs. Or maybe the Cricut Wild Card cartridge is another one of your Cricut cartridges so you can make a Filigree Easter Egg card. One of my Cricut Card suggestions is if you have your Imagination Cartridge on the Cricut Extension. You can make a card in a basket with a Bunny coloring the Easter eggs or a bunny. As far as all the Cricut card ideas I could come up with for Easter are concerned, they do not all need to have bunnies or eggs on them. Here is an example of using another of your Cricut cartridges, A Walk in My Garden cartridge. You can use this Cricut cartridge to make beautiful daffodils, hyacinths, or tulips to be your card theme. You are the Easter card maker, show off your talent, and have fun.

Then there's Mother's Day, the next big card day. Think of how your Mom would feel her child receiving a personalized greeting card. You are going to make her day entirely. Using your wonderful Cricut cutting machine, no matter what Cricut cartridges you have, you will be able to find something that will put a smile on her face, and of course you will do all this. It could be as simple as a basic flower from the cartridge of the Plantin School Book that you cut on a card in different sizes and layers, and then add the words Happy Mother's Day or the Best Mommy in the World. The best thing about your Cricut cutting machine is that it gives you thousands of Cricut card ideas and all the Cricut cartridges that are available to you. You can see your cards look so good that you cannot wait to send them out or start selling them. I'm going to get busy making my very own Cricut cutting machine with my handmade greeting cards, how about you?

## What is the Imagine Cricut Machine?

One of its kind is the Cricut Imagine machine which ProvoCraft publicized at the CHA. It is currently the only machine that allows the user to use the same device to both cut and print, saving a lot of time and money. With HP inkjet printing technology, you can select a pattern from a vast cartridge collection, get it printed and cut it in one go.

## To Scrapbookers, What Does It Mean?

A great way to improve and add pizzazz to all kinds of arts and crafts projects, including scrapbooking and card making, is to use cut-outs and shapes in different colors. These diets that are also called that consist of a variety of materials such as paper, foils, card stock, transparencies vellum, and thin plastics. Today, with most labor-intensive and automated cutters on the marketplace, examples are the Sizzix and Cricut Expression, you need to prepare ahead and select your die-cut color before cutting. In other words, the color of your design will be the color of your choice of paper (or cloth, or stock). Besides that, you may need to change paper colors frequently when creating complex or intricate designs.

Other systems, like the Wishblade, allow you to print the desired shape using an ordinary inkjet printer instead of running the printed page through the cutting machine. The biggest problem with that is that it's a two-step process, using two different machines, which requires the user to set up registration marks correctly so that the machine knows exactly where to cut. This is often a process of trial and error, and the outcomes are not always satisfactory. Thus, there is a need for a program that allows the user to print an image without manual registration and cut the image. This is where the Cricut Imagine comes in to fill a huge market gap and generally open up a whole new world of possibilities for scrapbookers, card makers, and paper craftsmen.

**Primary Features of Cricut Imagine**

- You can fill any form with beautiful patterns with Cricut Pattern and Cricut Color Cartridges, by adding.
- The designs have more dimension and variety.
- You can use all preceding Cricut Imagine cartridges. But new cartridges will also be released to operate exclusively

with this new unit, as was the case by means of the Cricut Cake.
- Cricut Imagine also supports equally the Gypsy and Design Studio software.
- Use of an LCD touch-screen navigation system to easily access all the information.
- New Cricut Imagine cartridges include: 12 new Cricut Imagine Art cartridges and 12 new Cricut Imagine Colors & Model cartridges.
- The paint and pattern generator on-board help you to choose colors, sizes, and more.
- The Cricut Imagine machine will cut shapes from .25" to 11.5" and works up to 12" x 12" large-format papers.
- Like Cricut and other previous devices, the Imagine doesn't require a device to operate.
- Share the same blade and blade housing as other Cricut types of machinery, making it relaxed for users to advancement short of having to purchase it all over again.
- Mat, which is significantly improved, is the only difference.

That means no more purchasing loads of costly scrapbook paper, changing colors of paper between cuts, or dealing with manual registration marks. Everything you need in one simple system to use that does everything for you and allows your creativity to soar. The Cricut Imagine is unique, not only to the art industry, but also to the technology community. There is currently no other tool that embodies both printings and cutting the way the image does.

# Chapter 2. List Of Materials That Can Be Used With Compatible Cricut Machines

Certain materials can be cut on various Cricut machines, but it does vary from machine to machine. The newer machines have more functionality with more materials. No matter the machine though, there are some materials you may have thought of, like those listed on the Cricut website, while there are others you may not have thought of. Just like you may not have thought of some out-of-the-box ideas for projects to do!

## Main Materials

Cricut Website is a treasure-trove of information for both the new and experienced Cricut user. One helpful feature is the list and store for materials. The items listed for sale on the website include:

- Cling for windows
- Washi sheets
- Vinyl
- Vellum

- Transfer Tape
- Poster board
- Iron-on materials
- Foils
- Leather-like materials
- Craft foam
- Papers, including cardstock
- Etc.

Within these categories, multiple items are also listed. For example, under vinyl, items are included like basic vinyl, transfer vinyl, and adhesive vinyl. Ultimately, the Cricut website lists over 100 different materials that the machines can cut, many of which they sell on the site. This is very convenient if you want to guarantee the materials will work with the machine and you do not want to waste their time shopping around for things.

Other people prefer to try more out-of-the-box materials and projects to test their creative powers and those of their machines.

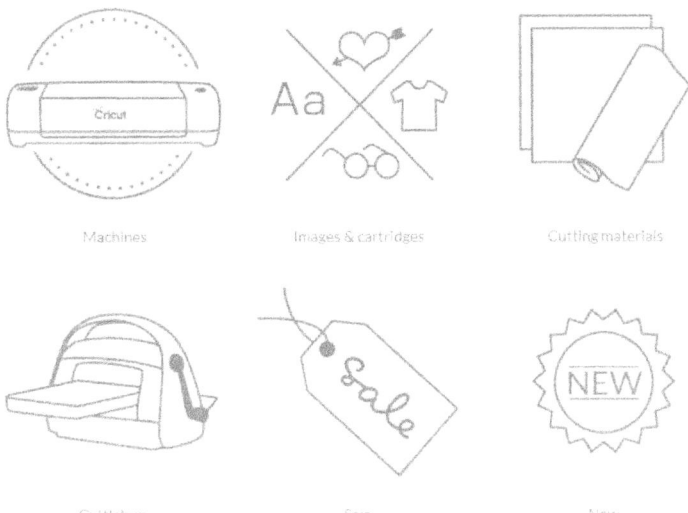

## Alternative Materials

While vinyl and paper are the most popular materials to cut with your Cricut, that material is just the "tip of the iceberg," so to speak. There are so many other materials crafters have used successfully with their Cricut machines. Below is a list of some of the items to consider:

- Balsa Wood

Balsa is a quick-growing, American tree. The thin wood it produces is often used in model making or rafts. This is because it is very lightweight and slightly pliable. Craft projects from balsa wood include favor tags for weddings or parties, rustic-looking placeholders for the table, or a natural-themed sign for a door or wall.

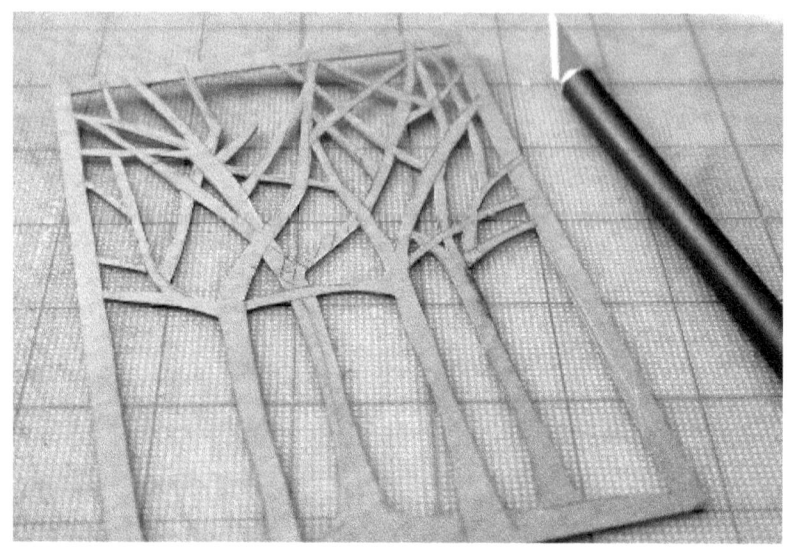

- Pens

While this is not exactly an unusual material, it is an often-under-used tool. These pens can not only be functional but can create beautiful sketches.

For some projects, a pen can be used to include creating coloring pages, placemat designs for children at restaurants or holidays (of course, these are great for adults, too!), or monogrammed jewelry. For example, a metallic initial can be printed on a circular piece of leather and strung on a necklace for an instant, personal statement piece of jewelry.

A mandala made with a pen and paper

- Duct Tape

The popularity of duct tape as a fashion or crafting item has blossomed over the past few decades, producing projects from wallets to prom dresses. It is still a material that some Cricut DIYers underestimate.

This material can be durable and fashionable. Projects made using Duct Tape include Bold and textured gift tags for packages or an art portfolio that showcases the vibrancy and precision of the artist with the added touch of this material.

- Fabric

Fabric is not an unusual material for some Cricut users, but because the variety of fabric available to choose from is so vast, it needs to be mentioned again because there are some techniques and materials that are a little more unusual. For example, cutting a lace-like pattern into fabrics can immediately add a color palette of fancy lace to any project. This also makes it possible to have the same lace pattern on a variety of complimentary fabrics or colors.

- Faux Leather and Leather

Cricut does not sell real leather. They offer a variety of different leather-like or "faux" leathers. "Faux" means "fake".

Depending on your preference, you can use either material. Despite what you choose, both are good materials to cut with the Cricut. Custom jewelry, like necklace pendants or earrings, are simple and stunning projects. These make beautiful and personal gifts or add the right touch to a special outfit. Leather can also be used for making fashionable bracelets or cuffs.

Having an intricate cut on a lovely piece of leather or faux leather, the bracelet can be attached to an adjustable band. Hair bows or bows to add to clothing or handbags are also possible. For a hair bow, hot glue a hair clip to the back when the bow is finished. Use hot glue or another adhesive to attach the bow to clothing or a purse. Other hair accessories can be made, like flowers and other shapes.

These can be attached to hair clips, like the bows, or attached to hard or stretchy headbands. Leather can also be used as an embellishment to pillows or other fabrics, like chair backs, or made into manly coasters.

- Felt

Felt is another multi-functional material that you can use for a host of projects. Because this item is fairly sturdy but has good flexibility, it is perfect for just about anything.

In addition, it comes in all different colors and is relatively inexpensive. Some unique projects that can be made from felt include garlands of multi-layered flowers to hang over a window curtain or above a bed, a textured phrase attached to a pillow, an interactive tree-shaped advent calendar, banners, ornaments, and cupcake or cake toppers.

- Magnets

Magnets can be used for more than just the fridge, and thankfully Cricut is there to help create new and fun ways to make magnets for all these different purposes. Be selective about the type of magnet you choose to cut.

Thick and solid magnets do not work well for these projects, but the thinner sheets of magnets are good for fun crafts.

Some ideas that are outside the fridge-box include; a magnet to be attached to the dishwasher that indicates if the machine is loaded with dirty or clean dishes, magnetic busy boards such as a mermaid scene with underwater characters or a race track with cars and spectators (do not forget a trophy for the first across the finish line!). Magnetic words to spell out messages on the side of the car or, yes, on the fridge, or school pride or mascots to attach to the car.

- Cling vinyl for windows

Custom decals for holidays or to create a statement on the car or a mirror can cost a lot of money if it is bought from a store or ordered custom from a shop.

Instead, use your Cricut to get crafty. Consider making a saying or image and stick it to the window.

# Chapter 3. Materials For Cricut Machines

Cricut machines have been designed to handle a wide variety of materials. Most of the machines can work with a majority of materials, but they do have specialties among them. Read on for more information on the Cricut Explore One, Cricut Explore Air 2, Cricut Maker, and Cricut EasyPress 2 and the materials that work best with each.

**Cricut Explore One**

This machine only has one carriage, so you might find yourself swapping out tools more often than with the other machines. This machine can cut over 100 different materials. It can also write and score. Here's a sampling of some of the most common materials used with the Explore One machine.

- Vinyl—Vinyl, outdoor vinyl, glitter vinyl, metallic vinyl, matte vinyl, stencil vinyl, dry erase vinyl, chalkboard vinyl, adhesive foils, holographic vinyl, printable vinyl, vinyl transfer tape, iron-on vinyl, glitter iron-on vinyl, foil iron-on, holographic iron-on, printable iron-on for light or dark fabric, flocked iron-on vinyl, and neon iron-on vinyl

- Paper—Cardstock, glitter cardstock, pearl paper, poster board, scrapbook paper, vellum, party foil, cereal boxes, construction paper, copy paper, flat cardboard, flocked cardstock and paper, foil embossed paper, freezer paper, kraft board, kraft paper, metallic cardstock and paper, notebook paper, paper grocery bags, parchment paper, paper board, pearl cardstock and paper, photographs, mat board, rice paper, solid core cardstock, watercolor paper, and wax paper
- Fabric—Burlap, canvas, cotton, denim, duck cloth, faux leather, faux suede, felt, flannel, leather, linen, metallic leather, oilcloth, polyester, printable fabric, silk, and wool felt
- Specialty—Adhesive foil, adhesive wood, aluminum sheets, aluminum foil, balsa wood, birch wood, corkboard, corrugated paper, craft foam, duct tape, embossable foil, foil acetate, glitter foam, magnet sheets, metallic vellum, paint chips, plastic, sticker paper, shrink plastic, stencil material, tissue paper, temporary tattoo paper, transparency film, washi sheets and tape, window cling, wood veneer, and wrapping paper

## Cricut Explore Air 2

The Explore Air 2 can cut the same materials as the Explore One. The difference is that it has two carriages instead of one, so it's easier to swap between tools. It's also a bit faster than Explore

One. The Air machines have wireless and Bluetooth capabilities, so you can use the Cricut Design Space on your phone, tablet, or laptop without connecting directly to the machine.

## Cricut Maker

The Cricut Maker has about 10x the cutting power of the Explore machines. It includes a rotary blade and a knife blade, so in addition to all the above materials, it can cut into more robust fabrics and materials. With the sharper blades, it's also better at cutting into more delicate materials without damaging them. Here's a list of some of the additional materials the Maker can cut.

- Acrylic felt
- Bamboo fabric
- Bengaline
- Birch
- Boucle
- Broadcloth
- Burlap
- Velvet
- Calico
- Cambric
- Canvas
- Carbon fiber
- Cashmere
- Challis
- Chambray
- Chantilly lace
- Charmeuse satin
- Chiffon
- Chintz
- Chipboard
- Corduroy
- Crepe paper
- Cutting mat protector
- Dotted Swiss
- Double cloth
- Double knit
- Dupioni silk
- EVA foam
- Eyelet
- Faille
- Fleece
- Foulard
- Gabardine
- Gauze
- Gel sheet
- Georgette
- Gossamer
- Grois point
- Habutai
- Heather
- Heavy watercolor paper
- Homespun fabric
- Interlock knit
- Jacquard
- Jersey
- Jute
- Kevlar
- La Coste
- Lycra
- Mesh
- Metal
- Microfiber
- Moleskin
- Monk's cloth
- Muslin
- Nylon
- Organza

- Handmade paper
- Plush
- Sailcloth
- Satin silk
- Seersucker
- Sequined cloth
- Bonded silk
- Tafetta
- Tulle
- Tweed
- Velvet
- Wool crepe

## Cricut EasyPress

The Cricut EasyPress 2 is a small, convenient heat press. It works with any type of iron-on material and can adhere to fabrics, wood, paper, and more. Cricut also offers Infusible inks that are transferred to the material using heat. The EasyPress is a great alternative to iron, as it heats more quickly and more evenly.

## Crafting Blanks

The objects you decorate using your Cricut can be referred to as blanks. This can be absolutely any object, and it can be something you stick vinyl to, etch, paint, draw on, write on, or anything else you can think of. They're called blanks because they provide a mostly blank surface to be decorated, though they can also have colors or designs.

Some popular blanks are cups, mugs, wine or champagne glasses, travel mugs, tumblers, and other such drinking vessels. Craft stores will usually sell these, but you can find them at almost any store. They don't need to be considered a "craft" supply for you to use. Most stores have a selection of plain cups and mugs or travel mugs and tumblers with no designs on them. As long as you can imagine a Cricut project with it, it's fair game.

Drink wares aren't the only kitchen or dining-related blanks. Get creative with plates, bowls, and serving utensils. Find blank placemats or coasters at most stores. Decorate mason or other types of jars. Dry goods containers, measuring cups, food storage containers, pitchers, and jugs—anything you can put in your kitchen can serve as a great blank for your projects.

Clothing is another popular choice for Cricut projects. T-shirts are easy to make with iron-on vinyl, and you can find cheap blanks at any store or a larger selection at craft stores. In fact, craft stores will typically have a large selection of clothing blanks, such as t-shirts, long sleeve shirts, ball caps, plain white shoes, plain bags, and so on. Thrift stores or consignment shops can be an unusual option as well. You could find a shirt with an interesting pattern that you'd like to add an iron-on to or something similar.

Glass is fun to work with and has a ton of project options with your Cricut machine. Glass blocks can be found at craft or hardware stores. Many stores that carry kitchenware will have plain glass cutting boards, or you can find them online. Craft stores and home goods stores could sell glass trinkets or décor that you can decorate. You can even buy full panes of glass at your local hardware store and have them cut it to your desired size.

There are plenty of blanks related to electronics, as well. Electronics stores, online stores, and some craft stores offer phone and tablet case blanks. They might be clear, white or black, or colored. Portable battery packs are another option as well. Many times, these blanks are significantly cheaper than already decorated ones, or you can buy them in bulk for a lower price. Get your phone case for a cheaper price and customize it how you like.

Book covers make great blanks, as well. Customize the cover of a sketchbook, notebook, or journal. Repair the cover of an aged book, or create a new book cover for a plain one that you have. If you have old books that you aren't going to read, create a new fake cover for them and use them as décor.

# Chapter 4. Easy Cricut Project Ideas

**DIY Leather Cuff**

***The Materials:***

You do not need many materials for this project. All you need to create your own DIY leather bracelet is:

- A minor piece of leather.
- A rope or cord.
- Curved nose pliers for jewelry (or old classic fine nose pliers also works!).
- Deep cut blade for your Cricut Explore.
- Small jump rings (2) (optional).

To develop the design, I selected an image of the concept space that I was looking for "lace." I had fun with the size and cut on the paper to check its size before cutting the most expensive skin. After reaching the perfect size, I pressed cut. My stomach may have flip flops while I was waiting!

I have to be completely honest here. I was hurt when I took the rug. The design, which was a bit complex, was cut perfectly everywhere. I didn't need to touch a single cut. (The only that can be carried out differently next time is to put the smooth side of the leather on the carpet so that the fibers of the fabric do not adhere to the carpet when the skin is removed!)

**DIY Leather Bracelet**

Once the pattern is cut, simply make the size of your cord or chain for the bracelet. I used 6 links on every side of the pattern and included the chain to the skin with small jump rings. You can tie the links directly to the skin, but my ties were very rigid and they didn't want to tear the skin to try and move. The jump rings were much more flexible.

## *How to Cut Leather with Cricut Explore:*

To cut the skin with Cricut Explore, you must have:

- A Cricut Explore Air or Cricut Explore One
- Cross transfer belt
- Cross hatch
- Leather tools (this is my favorite type of leather for fabrication because it is sturdy and fits perfectly, but you can also use other types of leather for this project).

Instead, we will use Cricut Transfer as a buffer between the leather and the cutting mat. It's a pretty easy and fast addition that will save you money and frustration.

Cut the transfer tape to the size of your skin, then glue it on the skin part. Finally, place it on the cutting mat with the transfer tape as a cushion.

Once you've loaded the skin into your machine, be sure to set the selector to "Custom". You can select "Skin Group" from the drop-down menu.

For my project, I used some leather keys with my own sources, as well as free forms of Cricut Design Space. We just created letters, reproduced one of the letters, and then soldered with a rectangle.

Once the cut is complete, you can peel off the transfer tape and reveal a clean tapestry cap underneath. No more pieces of skin ruining your carpet

**Leather Keychain**

Now that you've cut your leather, it's time to put in your key!

You will need:

- Leather Monogram
- Small talk
- Leather glue
- Bull clips (not shown)

Pass one side of the leather monograms onto the key ring, then fold the leather in half and remove each side with leather glue. Use bull sleeves to hold the sides together until the glue is completely dry.

Add some color to your keys with acrylic leather paint. I created a color inlay effect to embed a diagonal band with washi tape.

## Cutting of custom material

For the custom bass wood configuration, I made a cutting pressure of 220 and a multiple cavity of 4x. Important Tips! Be sure to reflect your image in the drawing space before cutting. The raft wood is a very red wood and the white rolls leave traces in the wood. When reflecting on the image, you can use the back that will be nice and smooth!

The cards came out very clean this time!

## Wood Raft Paper

So, I have all my letters once my size is finished and ready to put on my canvas. (I used an 18 x 24" black cloth.

## The Design

I used homemade acrylic paint and a sample paint remover to paint the letters of agglomerates. The "BE" received a layer of white paint and I left the wood letters on the tray.

## Painting Paper

I love the contrasting colors of the bright colors in black and white and it harmonizes with the colors I have in the room.

## 3D Letters

Once all the letters were in place, I glued them onto the fabric with hot glue. I couldn't be happier with the end result!

3D Literature Sign: Have Courage, be Kind

Playroom Beware: It really illuminates the children's study area and combines with DIY magnetic tangrams on the wall.

## Cricut Iron-On Picnic Blanket

Make your own round blanket with bright palm leaf details.

Starting with today's Cricut Ironing Picnic Blanket, which contains one of the latest images available in the Cricut Design Space Access service. As soon as I saw this Monstera leaf, he knew he was going to do something about it.

Use your Cricut Explore to create this Iron Cricut Smooth Cricut with vibrant and modern colors

Here's what you'll need:

- Explore Cricut
- Subscription to Cricut Design Space Access (optional, but excellent)
- Iron the shapes of Monstera leaves in bright colors with Cricut fuse material (I used wheat, raspberry, pink blush, lime, and sun yellow).
- 70" round white tablecloth

- Pom-pom trim
- Canvas glue
- Iron game
- Iron

Use your Cricut Explorer to create this brightly colored Cricut picnic blanket.

### Step 1

Fold the coat in half, this will make the job easier. Arrange all the crowd shapes as you want in the final drawing.

Use your Cricut Explore to create this Iron Cricut Smooth Cricut with vibrant and modern colors

### Step 2

Iron each shape slowly pays attention to the intersection of the shapes to avoid accidentally injuring one shape on the plastic support of the other.

### Step 3

I turn the tablecloth and use the fabric to glue the tassel thread over the entire edge of the tablecloth. Leave to dry for a few hours.

### Tips for Using Iron Materials

For all the shapes that come out of the edge, fold it under and iron on the bottom of the coat

Don't use steam! Use a dry hot iron to iron any shape.

Use your Cricut Explore to create this Iron Cricut Smooth Cricut with vibrant and modern colors.

## Glitter Monogram Cushion DIY

What you need:

- Cricut Explore Air Machine
- Cricut design space cost
- Iron Cricut in the color/style of your choice
- Cricut instruments
- iron
- table
- Scissors
- The rule of thumb/tape
- insert cushion
- pillow

1. Take your table and measure. Determine the desired size for your monogram to find out what size to get in my design space. My pillow measured 18 inches square (from the H&M store, nice and affordable things!), and I decided to make my monogram no more than 10 inches.
2. Begin by making your own monogram in the Cricut design space. I made my design with the Monogram KK font from the DaFont website. The best thing is it is free! You can download it here. Write the letters of your monogram with the text tool and select the Monogram KK character. And

then select Isolated Letters. This will ensure that your 3 letters are separate so that you can move and resize independently.

3. Put your letters to the desired size. For my monogram, I made our last initial (B) larger, 8 inches high. I made our first initials (E and J) every 6 inches tall. I put a 10 × 10 frame on my canvas to keep a reference to the height or width of the template. I like the appearance of these monograms when the letters overlap and interchange. So, I made sure each letter was played or overlapped in one way or another.

4. Once I appreciated my design, I selected the 3 levels of letters and clicked on Weld. This makes it possible to combine all overlapping edges into one large piece!

5. Now they are ready to cut! Make sure you remove or hide your square path if you created it to guide you. Click on the green IR button in the upper right corner of the design space to create your project. It looks like this:
Cricut GO button
The Cricut program puts the drawing on a page so you can cut the project. Be sure to select "Picture mirror (on the rail)" on the next panel.

6. Put the iron on the equipment on your Cricut cutting mat. Place the non-matte or glossy or colored sideways on the side of the rug. For my mission, I select the shiny silver material. Be sure to select Iron on the dial of your Cricut

machine. Then click on IR on your Cricut and see its magic!

7. After you cut your template, carefully remove any items that are not part of your template using your Cricut tools or your fingers. My design was very ornate and this part took a while. Be sure that you are inside a room that is well lit to see what you are doing. After removing all the unnecessary parts, you will be ready to stretch!

8. Warm up the iron and iron your model on the pillow, using a piece of cloth to protect it from the iron and your gift pattern. I used a Turkish towel, but you can wear an old shirt or whatever you have on hand.

   My pillow was a smooth and shiny material and took a little longer to look longer than I expected. I had to turn over my iron for planting. Imagine that each type of fabric is different, so keep that in mind when making your project.

   Each time during ironing, I took the fabric and started removing it from the adhesive panel. If he still employed his employer, he would accompany him again. Just keep on booting until your design adheres! Once everything is glued, remove the entire adhesive style.

# Chapter 5. Paper-Based Projects

**Christmas Greeting Cards**

You may have been aware before now that there are 50,000+ predesigned images in the Cricut Design Space library and Christmas is by the corner. Therefore, you have a lot of activities marking the season. Greeting cards are a great way to show that you care especially for your friends and family. The images in the library can create super amazing Christmas greeting cards you can send as gifts and for sales during Christmas.

Knowing there are many images you can play in the library is one thing, the other thing is knowing how to use these images to create beautiful and super amazing greeting cards with your Cricut Explore Air 2 machine. I want to show you how you can use your Cricut Explore Air 2 machine to do this using this step by step approach.

The materials for this project include a Cricut Explore Air 2 machine, computer or smartphone, cardboard papers, glue, a pair of scissors, Cricut writing pens, and micro glaze.

I want to believe that you know what Micro Glaze is but if you don't know, Micro glaze is a protective cream wax for coating art works especially papers. Since this project involves papers majorly, Micro glaze is important to produce a colorful print out with a little shine on it.

1. Go to your Design space app. open it and log into your account.
2. Go to Insert Images, click it, and type 'cards' in the text field to view hundreds of free images.
3. Tap or click on Insert shapes then select Square.
4. Go to the edit panel and click the Unlock button to unlock it.
5. Select the size of the card you wish from the available sizes.
6. Click the Ok button.
7. To produce a card, you wish to fold, score line at the middle of the square. To score a line in the middle, click on the inserted images to select it and view the score line. Go to the top middle position of the square, click it and drag it down to the bottom line of the square. To make sure that the score line is at the middle of the square, draw a box over the score line, click the Align button at the top of the Canvas and then click Center.
8. Attach the score line to the square by selecting the square and the score line together, then click Attach in the Layer's panel. Do not be surprised if the shapes change color when

you select it. Blue color indicates that the shape is selected, otherwise, it is white.

9. Adjust the color of the square.
10. Again, select the shapes, unlock it, then drag it down till the shapes cover 50% of the square.
11. Adjust the shapes and colors on the square to your wish then move to the next step.
12. Click the Text button on the left pane to pop up a text box where you can input whatever text you wish, type 'Merry Christmas' in the text field, or any text that sends your desired message to the recipient
13. Highlight the text then edit the text size, fonts, shape, and other properties of the text as you wish on your screen. Alternatively, you can use the pre-designed cards in the Design Space, edit them to obtain the final image that tickles your fancy, especially when you don't have the time and energy to start your design from the beginning. The only challenge with this is that you cannot share the files with anyone when there are copyrighted images on it. If you must share, then adjust any shared images in your design.
14. Once you are satisfied with your design, click the "Make it" button on the top right corner of your screen to cut your design out.

15. Check the preview of your design on the virtual mat to see the arrangement on the mat. If you are satisfied with the arrangement, click Continue.
16. Place the color marker in the left compartment. To do this, open the clamp of accessory A, remove the cap of the marker, push the marker inside accessory A till a clicking sound is heard then clamp the accessory.
17. Place your cardboard paper on the mat and then load it into the machine.
18. Press the Load/Unload button then press the flashing Cricut button to start cutting your shape.
19. Repeat steps 15-17 for all the layers you designed. Note that an extra layer will be required for the outer cover of the card.
20. When you're done printing and cutting your design, remove from the mat gently so that the tiny details don't get messed up or broken.
21. Apply a little micro glaze on the printed surface to protect the printout.
22. Arrange the layers together inking the edges where necessary then fold the score line properly. Make sure that you apply glue to the printed paper before attaching it to the card.

**Christmas Tag**

Christmas gift tags have been around for a very long time and will still be around as long as Christmas is still being celebrated. It is a beautiful way to customize your Christmas gifts and very cheap to make. The step by step approach to making an amazing Christmas tag for the season is as follows:

1. Let me start with the materials for this project which include: Cricut Explore Air 2 machine, White cardstock, Cricut pen (.4 fine point tip), ribbon, and weeding tool.
2. Create a New Project in your Design Space.
3. Upload your images for the Christmas tag, text messages, snowflakes, or any designed image you wish to use on the tag unto your Canvas.
4. Resize your tag to your desired value. I want to believe you can do that? At the Layer's panel, remember?
5. Zoom the tag if the size is really small on the screen so that you don't strain your eyes trying to see your design.
6. Place your snowflake on the front of your Christmas tag then align it to the center horizontally.
7. Resize the snowflake appropriately to fit into your Christmas tag.
8. Slice the snowflake and repeat the same process for the Christmas text message.

9. Change the image to white and select the color of the Cricut pen to Black 0.4 tip.
10. Attach all of them and click on the Go button on top.
11. Turn your dial to custom and select "Cardstock Intricate Cuts 0.27mm."
12. Place your cardstock paper on the Standard Grip mat and then load the mat by pressing the power button on your Cricut Explore Air 2 machine.
13. Insert your fine 0.4 fine pen in accessory A and press the flashing Cricut button to begin the writing and cutting process.
14. When the machine finishes its job, unload the mat by pressing the Load/Unload button again.
15. Color any part of the text that needs adjustment because the Cricut Explore Air 2 machine will not color the font for you.
16. Use a weeding tool to gently remove your Christmas tag from the mat.
17. Finally, use the ribbons to tie the Christmas tag to your desired position on your handcraft wall, or door, or any position you wish to place it in your house.

The good thing about the Christmas tag project is that you have the freedom to add any image of your choice to give it a personal message and appeal. Of course, it is super simple to do and will encourage you on to share the love this Christmas season.

## Monogrammed Christmas Ornament

A monogram is an image made by combining two or more overlapping graphemes or other letters to form one symbol or logo. A monogram is a unique way to give identity to the owner of a property which is something we all like to do. Of course, we all have properties in different forms, and what better way to find them than a monogram customized using your darling Cricut Explore Air 2 machine.

The Cricut Explore Air 2 machine can engrave monograms on materials including acrylic ornaments. These beautiful pieces of ornaments are beautiful to behold and gives the crafter such an amazing feeling of satisfaction and creativity.

The tools required for this project include Cricut Explore Air 2 machine, Chomas Creations Engraving Tool, Cricut Design space, a piece of an acrylic coaster, and painter's tape.

The Chomas Engraving Tool is used to engrave and etch materials with the help of a die cutting machine like your darling Cricut Explore Air 2. It is the second most important material for this project and it is easy to install on your Cricut Explore Air 2 machine.

Chomas Engraving Tool

Use the step by step approach described below to engrave your monogram on an acrylic coaster. It is super simple and will serve as amazing decorations for your room during the Christmas celebration and even as a gift to family and friends.

1. Select a monogram in Design Space and insert it into Canvas
2. Insert a circle into the Canvas or any proper shape for this project, but the circle will be preferably considering the shape of the ornament.
3. Weld the shapes into one color.
4. Set the size of the shape to that of the ornament plate you wish to use.
5. Place the monogram into the circle and resize the monogram to fit into the circle in a way that appeals to you.
6. To cut the coaster, send the design to the virtual mat and make sure that your design is in the right place where you wish Cricut Explore Air 2 machine to cut on the coaster, then use the next steps I to h to cut the coaster.
7. Set the coaster on the Strong Grip mat at the right place and secure it.
8. Load the mat by pressing the Load/Unload button on the machine.
9. Press the flashing 'C' Cricut button to start cutting the coaster.

10. When the cutting is done, press the Load/Unload button to unload the mat and remove the coaster that has been cut from the mat.
11. The next thing is to set the cut coaster unto the mat again at the precise position, then secure it firmly with painter's tape. Of course, the painter's tape should be underneath the coaster.
12. Replace the cutting blade with the Chomas engraving tool on the right-hand side of the adaptive tool. Make sure the coaster material is not touching the White Star Wheel while the machine is engraving it.
13. Repeat steps 2-3.
14. Finally, press the Load/Unload button to unload the mat showing your beautifully engraved monogram on the coaster.
15. Clean up by wiping dirt off the ornament, then hang it in your preferred place.

# Chapter 6. Cricut Projects With Vinyl

**Giant Vinyl Stencils**

Vinyl stencils are a good thing to create, too, but they can be hard. Big vinyl stencils make for an excellent Cricut project, and you can use them in various places, including bedrooms for kids.

You only need the Explore Air 2, the vinyl that works for it, a pallet, sander, and of course, paint and brushes. The first step is preparing the pallet for painting, or whatever surface you plan on using this for.

From here, you create the mermaid tail (or any other large image) in Design Space. Now, you will learn immediately that big pieces are hard to cut and impossible to do all at once in Design Space.

What you do is a section of each design accordingly, and remove any middle pieces. Next, you can add square shapes to the image, slicing it into pieces so that it can be cut on a cutting mat that fits.

At this point, you cut out the design by pressing "Make It", choosing your material, and working in sections.

From here, you put it on the surface that you are using; piecing this together with each line. You should have one image, after piecing it all together. Then, draw out the line on vinyl, and then paint the initial design. For the second set of stencils, you can simply trace the first one, and then paint the inside of them. At this point, you should have the design finished. When done, remove it very carefully.

And there you have it! Bigger stencils can be a bit of a project since it involves trying to use multiple designs all at once; but with the right care and the right designs, you will be able to create whatever it is you need to in Design Space, so you can get the results you are looking for.

**Cricut Quilts**

Quilts are a bit hard to do for many people, but did you know that you can use Cricut to make it easier? Here, you will learn an awesome project that will help you do this. To begin, you start with the Cricut Design Space. Here, you can add different designs that work for your project. For example, if you are making a baby blanket, or quilt with animals on it, you can add little fonts with the names of the animals, or different pictures of them, too. From here, you want to make sure you choose the option to reverse the design. That way, you will have it printed on correctly. At this point, make your quilt. Do various designs and sew the quilt as you want to.

From here, you should cut it on the iron-on heat transfer vinyl. You can choose that, and then press "Cut." The image will then cut into the piece.

At this point, it will cut itself out, and you can proceed to transfer this with some parchment paper. Use an EasyPress for best results and push it down. There you go, an easy addition that will definitely enhance the way your blankets look.

## Cricut Unicorn Backpack

If you are making a present for a child, why not give them some cool unicorns? Here is a lovely unicorn backpack you can try to make. To make this, you need ¾ yards of a woven fabric—something that is strong, since it will help with stabilizing the backpack. You will also need half a yard of quilting cotton for the lining. The coordinating fabric should be around about an eighth of a yard. You will need: about a yard of fusible interfacing, some strap adjuster rings, a zipper that is about 14 inches and does not separate, and some stuffing for the horn.

1. To start, you will want to cut the main fabric; you should use straps, the loops, a handle, some gussets for a zipper, and the bottom and side gussets.
2. The lining should be done too, and you should make sure you have the interfacing. You can use fusible flex foam, to help make it a little bit bulkier.

3. From here, cut everything and then apply the interfacing to the backside. The flex-foam should be adjusted to achieve the bulkiness you are looking for. You can trim this, too. The interfacing should be on the backside; then add the flex foam to the main fabric. The adhesive side of this will be on the right-hand side of the interfacing.
4. Fold the strap pieces in half and push one down, on each backside. Halve it, and then press it again; stitch these closer to every edge, and also along the short-pressed edge, as well.
5. From here, do the same thing with the other side, but add the ring for adjustment, and stitch the bottom of these to the main part of the back piece.
6. Then add them both to the bottom.
7. At this point, you have the earpieces that should have the backside facing out. Stitch, then flip out and add the pieces.
8. Add these inner pieces to the outer ear, and then stitch these together.
9. At this point, you make the unicorn face in the Design Space. You will notice immediately when you use this program that everything will be black, but you can change this by adjusting the desired layers to each color. You can also just use a template that fits, but you should always mirror this before you cut it.

10. Choose vinyl, and then insert the material onto the cutting mat. From there, cut it and remove the iron-on slowly.

You will need to do this in pieces, which is fine because it allows you to use different colors. Remember to insert the right color for each cut. At this point, add the zipper, and there you go!

**Custom Back to School Supplies**

This tutorial will show you how to use your iPad to create and convert designs for your Cricut machine to cut!

*Materials needed:*

- Vinyl
- Standard Grip Mat
- White Paper
- Markers (including black)
- Pencil Case
- 3 Ring Binder
- iPad Pro (optional)
- Apple Pencil
- Cricut Design Space App
- Drawing app (e.g. ProCreate)
- ProCreate Brushes

*Instructions:*

1. The first thing to do is to convert your kid's drawing into an SVG file that the Cricut Design Space recognizes. This will be done by tracing it in the ProCreate app.
2. Get your child's design—it should not be too complex, to minimize weeding.
3. Open the Procreate app on your iPad.
4. Create a new canvas on ProCreate. Click on the "Wrench" icon and select "Image."
5. Next, click "Take a Photo." Take a picture of the design. When you are satisfied with the image, click "Use It."
6. On the Layer Panel (the two squares icon), add a new layer by clicking the "Plus" sign.
7. In the Layers panel, select the layer containing the picture and click the "N." Also, reduce the layer's opacity so that you can easily see your draw lines.
8. From your imported brushes, select the "Marker" brush. To avoid the need to import a brush, choose the inking brush. You can resize the brush in the brush settings under the "General" option.
9. On the new layer, trace over the drawing.
   a. Click on the "Wrench" icon, click "Share," then "PNG."
   b. Next, "Save" the image to your device.
   c. Alternately, use your black marker and trace the drawing on a blank piece of paper, then take a picture of it, using your iPad or phone.

d. The next stage is to cut the design out in Cricut Design Space
e. Open up the Cricut Design Space app on your iPad.
f. Create a 'New Project'.
g. Select "Upload" (located at the screen's bottom). Select "Select from Camera Roll" and select the PNG image you created in ProCreate or the image you traced out.
h. Follow the next steps.
i. Save the design as a cut file and insert it into the canvas. Here, you can resize the design or add other designs.
j. Next, click "Make It" to send it to your Cricut.
k. Choose "Vinyl' as the material.
l. Place the vinyl on the mat and use the Cricut to cut it.

10. Now, you can place the vinyl cutouts on the back, to make your child stand out!

**Gift Tags**

*Materials needed:*

- Cricut machine
- Variety of cardstock, and a vinyl
- A ready-made Design Space project, for tags that say 'I love you'
- Glitter pen of your choice
- Account for Design Space

*Instructions:*

1. Follow the prompts to draw, and then cut each layer as the project needs.
2. Glue two paper layers together. "Align" the heart-shaped hole at the top of the tag.
3. Add your vinyl, and then burnish it to make sure it will adhere properly, and thoroughly.
4. Add ribbon or twine to the hole, for the tag.

**Paper Pinwheels**

*Materials needed:*

- Cricut Maker or Cricut Explore
- Standard Grip mat
- Patterned cardstock in desired colors
- Embellishments
- Paper straws
- Hot glue

*Instructions:*

1. Log into the "Design Space" application and click on the "New Project" button on the top right corner of the screen to view a blank canvas.

2. Let us use an already existing project from the Cricut library and customize it. So, click on the "Project" icon and type in "Paper Pinwheel" in the search bar.
3. Click on "Customize" to further edit the project to your preference, or simply click on the "Make It" button and load the cardstock to your Cricut machine, and follow the instructions on the screen to cut your project.
4. Using hot glue, adhere the pinwheels together to the paper straws, and the embellishments as shown in the picture above.

**Rugrats T-shirt**

*The materials that you will need for this project are:*

- The Explore Air, or the Maker
- An iron
- A small piece of fabric or linen cloth
- T-shirts
- A Rugrats file (SVG file)
- Supplies from the Cricut company which are:
- Access membership
- The standard cutting mat
- Weeder
- Scissors
- An iron-on lite (vinyl)
- An iron-on glitter

*The instructions that you need to make this design are listed here:*

1. Open your design in the Design Space.
2. Choose a color scheme you want to use.
3. Attach your images to cut.
4. Place your vinyl onto the cutting mat, and be sure that the shiny side is down.
5. Load your mat into the machine.
6. Click the "Go" button to start the cutting process. Make sure that your image is mirrored. You will have to check the box that says "Mirror Image."
7. Weed your cut design.
8. Repeat the process with the different pieces of your images using different vinyl pieces to add color.
9. Place the image on the shirt how you want it to look.
10. Iron, be careful. Focus on the corners of your design. It should peel easily.

These shirts are a really great way for you to get creative and have fun. Does your child like unicorns or superheroes? You can do this, too! With the Cricut machine, you are only limited by your own creativity. There are thousands of designs that you can use for T-shirts: from movies, cartoons, anime, your favorite childhood characters, and anything else you can imagine including favorite animals and quotes.

# Chapter 7. Project To Create Fabric Cuts (Part 1)

**Adorable Christmas Tea Towels**

*Instructions:*

- I opened Cricut Design Space and began a fresh project. The Design Space Image Library has over 60,000 pictures, so it's simple to begin designing your project in no time.

- Press the image you want to work with and the software inserts it into a fresh project document. I chose these wonderful hand-lettered "Merry and Bright" and "Merry Christmas" designs for my towels and arranged them for vinyl heat transfer sheets.
- Explore Air's favorite features are dial settings.
- With Cricut Explore Air, you just turn the knob to grab stuff you're working with, and the machine looks after the straightforward peasy.
- Set the "Iron-on" dial, and you're prepared to cut.
- Place a sheet of vinyl heat transfer, load it into the device, and press the cut button.
- Use Cricut Weeder to remove the excess vinyl from the design.
- I put the vinyl on my folded tea towel, covered it with a cloth, and ironed it in the instructions of the package.
- Once the vinyl heat transfer has been strongly adhered to, and discard plastic backup.
- I slipped a piece of cardstock under the towel top and used silver, gold, and champagne-colored fabric paint to add some shiny polka dots. Allow the paint to dry completely before removing the paper layer below.

**Mommy Is on a Break "Socks"**

Using my Cricut to create these socks, I began opening the Cricut Design Space. I typed the sentences into the design, played the size, and spaced a bit until I was sure my socks fit.

Then I loaded the heat transfer vinyl into the Cricut and sent the Cricut the cutting design. Don't forget to mirror your iron-on image design, so the text isn't backward in your project.

While cutting the vinyl, I cut some dense paper to produce inserts for my clothes to help "spread them out" while ironing on the design. The inserts were about 3" wide and 7" long, and I put them down to the toe in my shoes, so the bottom was flat.

I removed the background vinyl once the vinyl was sliced, then placed the vinyl sentences on my socks' soles.

I used my iron vinyl heat-press, but you can use iron instead.

After pushing the vinyl onto the clothes, I let them cool for a minute, pull the inserts out, and put them on. These were a super comfortable couple of socks already.

**Fabric Heart Coasters Using Cricut Maker**

*Supplies:*

- Cricut Maker
- Cotton fabric with coordinating thread
- Fusible fleece Rotary cut and mat or
- Iron Sewing Machine

*Instructions:*

Step 1

- Cut fabric to 12" width to fit on the cutting board. If your fabric is longer than matting, no problem. It can hang the edge.

Step 2

- Open and add a fresh project. Click "forms" and insert a heart-shaped pop-up window.
- Reduce the heart to 5.5". Click the top-right corner "Make." Change "Project copies" to 4 in the top-left corner and click "Apply."
- Click "Continue" in the bottom right corner. Set the material to "Medium cotton."
- Load and cut the mat with the fabric.

Step 3

- Repeat Step Two, but this time put the fusible fleece on the cutting mat. You'll also alter the heart shape to 5,375. Click "View more" when choosing content and type "fusible fleece" in the search bar.
- Cut two fusible fleece hearts.

Step 4

- Attach a fusible fleece heart to the tissue core with a warm iron. Repeat the second fleece heart.

- Sew heart forms together to create fabric heart coasters with a Cricut.

Step 5

- Sew together two heart forms (one with a fleece attached). Leave a tiny gap in turning to stitch.

Step 6

- Clip the curves below.

Step 7

- Turn the heart right. Press warm iron fold opening corners and click again.

Step 8

- Heart stitch, edge 1/4''.
- Consider using two distinct fabrics, such as pink/white stripes and pink/white floral fabric. They're reversible after all.

## Cricut Iron Shirt on Vinyl

Making a T-shirt needs two significant measures. First, you must decide what to say. I recommend you attempt to stick with one color. Sayings, sentences, or words are ideal.

Second, you must take on which shirt you'd like the saying. I produced my lovely sister's "fries before guys" shirt. She went to Target and discovered her smooth, flowy blouse.

Make sure the shirt could be ironed because you're going to use an iron on it. Here are a few things you'll need: Cricut Explore Air 2, Iron-on Vinyl

How to Cut Iron-On Vinyl:

- You'll begin with your picture. You can upload an image from the computer or create an image in Cricut Design Space.
- Open Design Space Cricut.
- Choose your canvas by left-clicking "Canvas." It's a shirt type baseball tee, so I chose that. Set the shirt size under "Canvas" on the right.
- Left-click "Upload picture." By browsing your files, pick your image, and choose what it is. For this project, and most iron-on projects, select "Simple Cut."
- Now press the space you'd like to cut out. Remember every letter's inside. That's enjoyable for some reason. It brings me back to my Microsoft Paint days when I used Bucket. Remember this?
- The next step is crucial. (Most are essential, but it's simple to miss.) Select "Cut Image"—NOT "Print," then "Cut Image." (Printing is a distinct project form.) Place this picture on your canvas and size it to your liking.
- Place iron on the shiny side of your mat and turn the button to Iron-on, or select Iron-on from the drop-down menu.
- Click "Cut."
- Ok, that's another significant, easy-to-miss move. Click "Iron-On Mirror" before hitting "Go."

- After cutting, remove surplus vinyl around the edges. Use your weeding tool to remove the parts in letters.
- Customizing your t-shirt How to Iron on Vinyl to T-shirt Now iron it on. Set your iron to "Cotton," or the hottest environment. Ensure there's no steam.
- Start warming the material. Put iron on the shirt for 15 seconds.
- Place your iron-on vinyl wherever you want. Put a pure cotton cloth on top of the plastic. That's important, so you don't melt the plastic on your shirt.
- Put iron on the press cloth for about 30 seconds. Flip your jacket over, do the same thing across the shirt.
- Now you'll take the sticky portion and separate it from the vinyl. Do this while it's hot. It'll be much more straightforward. If a piece doesn't come off, place the iron on the portion you're attempting to pick up, and it should pull off.
- Now plastic should be separated from vinyl. Put the press cloth back on and run with the iron, so you know it's wonderful.

# DIY Striped Nautical Tote Bag

*Supplies:*

- Cricut
- Glitter Iron-On Vinyl in blue
- Fabric Medium DecoArt
- Americana Acrylic Craft Paint

*Instructions:*

Step 1

- Use a weeding tool to get rid of all the surplus vinyl around your anchor picture

Step 2

- Tape a striped pattern on the canvas tote bag

Step 3

- Mix one portion of the color medium with one part of the acrylic. Next, remove the painter's tape

Step 4

- Let the paint dry entirely, then use a warm iron. Alternatively, the brand new Cricut Easy Press to apply the glitter iron-on anchor picture.

**Tooth Fairy Pouch**

*Supplies:*

- Array of Pens
- Tons of products such as SportsFlex iron-on vinyl,

- Weeding tool
- Embossed foil paper,
- Also, holographic sparkle XL scraper

*Instructions:*

- Begin by opening a Blank Canvas in the Design Space.
- Kindly go to Images in the left Design Panel and search for the word "tooth." You can also check the file by typing in #M22992CA. It's the middle tooth in the screenshot below: then click on the face and white tooth spots in the Layers panel and delete them, leaving the gray piece.
- We'll cut the tooth in iron-on white vinyl, but using the gray layer makes it simpler to see what we're doing.
- Then, using the Design Panel text tool, type your child's name.
- Then we want to make this a Cricut font with a description. To do this, go to the font drop-down menu and right-click "Filter" and select "Multi-Layer." This will narrow your decisions down to more than one layer of fonts.
- Then pick the one you like. I chose Piper's Alphalicious Short Stack, Miles' Cherry Limeade. Change letter spacing if you think letters are too distant. Copy and paste a second name copy.
- In the Layers Panel, visualize the outline layer by pressing the "eye" icon.
- Then delete the primary font layer, leaving the outline.

- Then choose both name and tooth and click on "Slice" at the bottom of the Layers Panel. Slice the tooth and name.
- Delete the purple letters (there will be two—the portion of the letters outside the tooth and the portion of the letters inside the tooth. Then delete the gray messages, leaving you with an overview of the letters. Then insert the other name you recorded previously on top of the tooth to make sure everything fits together.
- Having your two parts adhered together you are done. I enjoy this project because Cricut Design Space is readily customizable—no additional files are needed.

**Leather Geometric Buffalo Pillow**

*Supplies:*

- Cricut Maker

- Cricut 12x 14"
- Cardstock Cricut
- Cutting Mat
- Cricut Fine Point Blade Glue or Tape Runner

*Instructions:*

- Use the connection above to resize the flowers to the size you need, then click "Make It."
- Once cut, you can collect any parts you want. I hotly attached my toothpicks to the top of my cake. For the term topper, I used bigger wood skewers to stand above the flowers. Instead of flowers, this would be super sweet with mini paper rosettes.
- Use paper and your Cricut maker to create custom cake decor. With every addition to the tools the maker utilizes, the Cricut Maker has already made it so much easier to create the possibilities.

# Customized Pillow with Cricut

*Supplies:*

- Protective Sheet Pillow Cover
- Cricut Machine
- Glitter Iron-On Vinyl
- Cricut EasyPress Mat
- Insert Cricut Access
- Iron-On

*Instructions:*

Step 1

- Open the Cricut Design Space on your smartphone. Click "New Project" from the Home tab.

Step 2

- Select the text icon at the lower part of the screen and choose your required font. Type your last name and drag the box corner to make it bigger or lower to suit your pillow

Step 3

- Next, pick the Text icon to insert a second line of text for your "Est. Year."
- Drag and center properly under your last name

Step 4

- Next, pick both textboxes simultaneously and press the attach button. Appears when you click the Actions button. This will connect the two text boxes for focused cutting.

Step 5

- Next press the "Make It" button, and the screen appears. You'll want to make sure the Mirror's "on."

Step 6

- To switch off and on the mirror environment, press the picture at the top left corner. The screen above appears. Switch "on."

Step 7

- Mirror button—The mat will now display your mirrored picture, and you're prepared to load your Iron-On Vinyl

SHINY SIDE DOWN onto your mat. Click and follow the prompts.

Step 8

- Once the design is sliced, weed the surplus vinyl and center your pillow cover design.

Step 9

- Next, set the EasyPress timer and temperature for your shirt material. Refer to EasyPress Settings Chart.

Step 10

- Cover the structure with the Iron-On Protective Sheet and top the protective sheet with the EasyPress and click the Cricut button. Remove once it's beeped. Flip through your pillow cover and heat back 10 to 15 seconds.

Step 11

- Cool the iron-on and merely remove the sheet.

# Chapter 8. Project To Create Fabric Cuts (Part 2)

Let's start these projects using fabric as the base material. You will learn to create a variety of projects that you can further customize as you follow the instructions below and have unique designs of your own.

**Fabric Headband**

Materials needed— "Cricut Maker" or "Cricut Explore", FabricGrip mat, gray polka dot fabric, thread, black or decorative elastic, home sewing machine.

- Click on the "Projects" icon and type in "fabric headband" in the search bar.
- Click on "Customize" to edit the project to your preference further or simply click on the "Make It" button and load the fabric to your "Cricut" machine by placing the right side down on the mat and follow the instructions on the screen to cut your project.
- For assembly, measure your head where you would wear the headband and minus 15 inches from the measurement

then cut the elastic at that length to use underneath the headband.
- Place the right sides together and pin the elastic inside with the ends sticking out that can be pinned at the end of the headband.
- Use the sewing machine to sew around the outside edge of the headband leaving a 0.5-inch seam. Then sew over the ends of the elastic while it is between the two headband pieces leaving 2 inches opening unsewn along one side of the headband.
- Clip around the seam allowances with snips and turn the headband right side out. Use the end of a spoon to turn the edges of the headband out then use an iron to press and solidify the shape.
- Top stitch around the edge of the headband with a quarter-inch seam allowance for a finished look and close the turning hole.

**Forever Fabric Banner**

Materials needed— "Cricut Maker" or "Cricut Explore", FabricGrip mat, glitter iron-on (black, pink), "Cricut EasyPress", weeder, pink ribbon, canvas fabric, sew able fabric stabilizer, sewing machine, and thread.

- Log into the "Design Space" application.

- Click on the "Projects" icon and type in "fabric banner" in the search bar.
- Click on "Customize" to edit the project to your preference further or simply click on the "Make It" button. Place the trimmed fabric on the cutting mat removing the paper backing then load it to your "Cricut" machine and follow the instructions on the screen to cut your project. Similarly, load the iron-on vinyl sheet to the "Cricut" and cut the design, making sure to mirror the image.
- Carefully remove the excess material from the sheet using the "weeder tool," making sure only the design remains on the clear liner.
- Using the "Cricut Easy Press Mini" and "Easy Press Mat" the iron-on layers can be easily transferred to the fabric. Preheat your "Easy Press Mini" and put your iron-on vinyl design on the fabric and apply pressure for a couple of minutes or more. Wait for a few minutes prior to peeling off the design while it is still warm.

**Fabric Flower Brooch**

Materials needed—"Cricut Maker" or "Cricut Explore", FabricGrip mat, printable iron-on, "Cricut EasyPress", weeder, fabric pencil pouch, and inkjet printer.

- Log into the "Design Space".

- Click on the "Projects" icon and type in "fabric pouch" in the search bar.
- Click on "Customize" to edit the project to your preference further or simply click on the "Make It" button and follow the prompts on the screen for using an inkjet printer to print the design on your printable vinyl and subsequently cut the design.
- Carefully remove the excess material from the sheet using the "weeder tool".
- Using the "Cricut Easy Press Mini" and "Easy Press Mat" the iron-on layers can be easily transferred to the fabric. Preheat your "Easy Press Mini" and put your iron-on vinyl design on the fabric and apply pressure for a couple of minutes. Wait for a few minutes before peeling off the design while it is still warm.

**Flower Brooch**

Materials needed—"Cricut Maker" or "Cricut Explore", FabricGrip mat, aqua fabric, liquid starch, iron and ironing board, brooch fastener, needle, ivory thread, button cover kit with wire loop back (size 20).

- Log into the "Design Space" application and click on the "New Project" button.

- Click on the "Projects" icon and type in "fabric brooch" in the search bar.
- Click on "Customize" to edit the project to your preference further or simply click on the "Make It" button.
- Prior to cutting the fabric, press the fabric pieces, and follow the instructions on liquid starch to prepare the material for the application. Place the fabric pieces with the printed sided down on the cutting mat, then load it to your "Cricut" machine and follow the instructions on the screen to cut your project.
- Use the button cover kit to cover one button and run a stitch along the center circle of the smallest flower. Then pull the thread to cinch in the center. Repeat this for the other flowers.
- Carefully layer the flowers together concentrically and stitch together in the center. Lastly, stitch the covered button to the center of the stitched flower, then stitch the brooch fastener to the back of the flower.

**Leather Flower Hat**

Materials needed—"Cricut Maker" or "Cricut Explore", standard grip mat, Cricut Faux Leather, button, strong adhesive, and hat.

- Log into the "Design Space" application and click on the "New Project" button on the top right corner of the screen to view a blank canvas.
- Click on the "Projects" icon and type in "leather flower hat" in the search bar.
- Click on "Customize" to edit the project to your preference further or simply click on the "Make It" button and load the faux leather to your "Cricut" machine by placing it face down on the mat and follow the instructions on the screen to cut your project.
- For assembly, glue tabs on each flower together to give shape to every single layer and let dry.
- Glue all the flower layers on top of one another with the biggest layer at the bottom. Once the flower dries completely, glue a button on the center of the flower. And finally, glue the flower to the hat.

**Floral Mousepad**

Materials needed—"Cricut Maker" or "Cricut Explore", FabricGrip mat, printable fabric, mousepad, adhesive.

- Log into the "Design Space" application and click on "New Project."

- Click on the "Images" icon on the "Design Panel" and type in "#MB145E" in the search bar. Select the image and click on the "Insert Images" button at the bottom of the screen.
- Edit the project to your preference or simply click on the "Make It" button and load the vinyl sheet to your "Cricut" machine and follow the instructions on the screen to print and cut your project.
- Once you have the printed fabric cut, use the adhesive to adhere it to the mousepad.

**Jellybean Burp Cloth**

Materials needed—"Cricut Maker" or "Cricut Explore", FabricGrip mat, fabric (light gray, teal), rotary cutter, turning tool, sewing machine, and thread.

- Click on the "Projects" icon and type in "jellybean burp cloth" in the search bar.
- Click on "Customize" to edit the project to your preference further or simply click on the "Make It" button. Place the trimmed fabric on the cutting mat then load it to your "Cricut" machine and follow the instructions on the screen to cut your project. (Pay attention to the direction of the print for each fabric piece).
- With the right sides together, pin the two bean pieces together and sew with a 6mm seam around the edge of the

bean pieces, leaving a 1-2-inch opening for turning in the middle straight area.
- Clip all curves generously and use a chopstick to turn the fabric pieces' right side out through the turning hole. Press all seams.
- Lastly, top stitch the entire shape and close the turning hole as well.

## Personalized Coaster Tiles

Materials needed—"Cricut Maker" or "Cricut Explore", standard grip mat, "Cricut" iron-on lite, freezer paper, "Cricut Easy Press Mini", "Easy Press" mat, weeding tool, pillow cover, screen print paint, paintbrush.

- Click on the "Images" icon on the "Design Panel" and type in "#MED91E0" in the search bar. Select the image and click on the "Insert Images" button at the bottom of the screen.
- Edit the project to your preference or simply click on the "Make It" button and load the freezer paper with the non-shiny side up on the mat to your "Cricut" machine and follow the instructions on the screen to cut your project.
- Using a weeder tool, remove the negative space pieces of the design. Carefully place the stenciled quote on the pillow.

- Using the "Cricut Easy Press Mini" and "Easy Press Mat", iron on the design to the pillow. Preheat your "Easy Press Mini" and put your design on the desired area and apply pressure for a couple of minutes or more. Remove the freezer paper and let it dry overnight.
- Set the paint with the "EasyPress" once again and enjoy your new pillow!

# Chapter 9. Project With Glass

Projects and Ideas with Glass Vinyl cut with your Cricut machine can help you create beautiful glass projects. There are several different ways you can use it, as well. Any glass object can be a blank for these projects. You might already have some things in your kitchen that you'd like to decorate. These make wonderful gifts, too—no one will believe that you made them yourself and that they're not expensive gifts.

Glass etching cream is an interesting product that lets you easily create etched glass projects. There are several different brands that you can find at craft stores or online. You may be able to find them at hardware stores as well.

Read the instructions carefully and follow them exactly, to get your desired results and to be safe. It is actually an acid that eats away at the glass to create the etched effect. This may vary between brands, but often, stirring the cream around during its setting time will make the etching more pronounced. This will be a permanent effect on the glass.

Besides etching, you can also create beautiful glass projects using vinyl.

Outdoor vinyl, which is permanent, is the best choice if you want the design to stay put through use and washing. Removable vinyl will be temporary, and you can peel it off; it won't survive being washed. Window-cling vinyl sticks to glass via static, so they are quite temporary but can easily be changed out and reused.

**Etched Monogrammed Glass**

Etched Monogrammed Glass Glasses are one of the most-used things in your kitchen, and it's impossible to have too many of them. It's actually quite easy to customize them with etching, and it will look as if a professional did it. Simply use glass etching cream that you can find at any craft store! Be sure to read the instructions and warning labels carefully before you begin. The vinyl will act as a stencil, protecting the parts of the glass that you don't want to etch. Be sure to take your time to get the vinyl smooth against the glass, especially where there are small bits. You don't want any of the cream to get under the edge of the vinyl. You can use the Cricut Explore One, Cricut Explore Air 2, or Cricut Maker for this project.

*Supplies Needed:*

- A glass of your choice—make sure that the spot you want to monogram is smooth
- Vinyl
- Cutting mat

- Weeding tool or pick
- Glass etching cream

*Instructions:*

1. Open Cricut Design Space and create a new project.
2. Select the "Image" button in the Design Panel and search for "monogram."
3. Select your preferred monogram and click "Insert."
4. Put the vinyl on your cutting mat.
5. Direct the project to your machine.
6. Utilize a weeding device or pick to remove the monogram, leaving the vinyl around it.
7. Remove the vinyl from the mat.
8. Carefully apply the vinyl around your glass, making it as smooth as possible, particularly around the monogram.
9. If you have any letters with holes in your monogram, carefully reposition those cutouts in their proper place.
10. Following the instructions on the etching cream, apply it to your monogram.
11. Remove the cream and then the vinyl.
12. Give your glass a good wash.

## Live, Love, Laugh Glass Block

Glass blocks are an inexpensive yet surprisingly versatile craft material. You can find them at both craft and hardware stores. They typically have a hole with a lid so that you can fill the blocks with the items of your choice. This project uses tiny fairy lights for a glowing quote block, but you can fill it however you'd like. The frost spray paint adds a bit of elegance to the glass and diffuses the light for a softer glow, hiding the string of the fairy lights.

Holographic vinyl will add to the magical look, but you can use whatever colors you'd like. This features a classic quote that's great to have around your house, but you can change it. You can use the Cricut Explore One, Cricut Explore Air 2, or Cricut Maker for this project.

*Supplies Needed:*

- Glass block
- Frost spray paint
- Clear enamel spray
- Holographic vinyl
- Vinyl transfer tape
- Cutting mat
- Weeding tool or pick
- Fairy lights


*Instructions:*

1. Spray the entire glass block with frost spray paint, and let it dry.

2. Spray the glass block with a coat of clear enamel spray, and let it dry.
3. Open Cricut Design Space and create a new project.
4. Select the "Text" button in the Design Panel.
5. Type "Live Love Laugh" in the text box.
6. Use the dropdown box to select your favorite font.
7. Arrange the words to sit on top of each other.
8. Place your vinyl on the cutting mat.
9. Send the design to your Cricut.
10. Use a weeding tool or pick to remove the excess vinyl from the design.
11. Apply transfer tape to the design.
12. Remove the paper backing and apply the words to the glass block.
13. Smooth down the design and carefully remove the transfer tape.
14. Place fairy lights in the opening of the block, leaving the battery pack on the outside.

**Unicorn Wine Glass**

Who doesn't love unicorns? Who doesn't love wine? Bring them together with these glittery wine glasses! The outdoor vinyl will hold up to use and washing, and the Mod Podge will keep the glitter in place for years to come.

Customize it even more with your own quote. You could use a different magical creature as well—mermaids go great with glitter too! Customize this to suit your tastes or to create gifts for your friends and family. Consider using these for a party and letting the guests take them home as favors! You can use the Cricut Explore One, Cricut Explore Air 2, or Cricut Maker for this project.

*Supplies Needed:*

- Stemless wine glasses
- Outdoor vinyl in the color of your choice
- Vinyl transfer tape
- Cutting mat
- Weeding tool or pick
- Extra fine glitter in the color of your choice Mod Podge

*Instructions:*

1. Open Cricut Design Space and create a new project.
2. Select the "Text" button in the Design Panel.
3. Type "It's not drinking alone if my unicorn is here."
4. Using the dropdown box, select your favorite font.
5. Adjust the positioning of the letters, rotating some to give a whimsical look.

6. Select the "Image" button on the Design Panel and search for "unicorn."
7. Select your favorite unicorn and click "Insert," then arrange your design how you want it on the glass.
8. Place your vinyl on the cutting mat, making sure it is smooth and making full contact.
9. Send the design to your Cricut.
10. Use a weeding tool or pick to remove the excess vinyl from the design. Use the Cricut BrightPad to help if you have one.
11. Apply transfer tape to the design, pressing firmly, and making sure there are no bubbles.
12. Remove the paper backing and apply the words to the glass where you'd like them. Leave at least a couple of inches at the bottom for the glitter.
13. Smooth down the design and carefully remove the transfer tape.
14. Coat the bottom of the glass in Mod Podge, wherever you would like glitter to be. Give the area a wavy edge.
15. Sprinkle glitter over the Mod Podge, working quickly before it dries.
16. Add another layer of Mod Podge and glitter, and set it aside to dry.
17. Cover the glitter in a thick coat of Mod Podge.
18. Allow the glass to cure for at least 48 hours.

# Chapter 10. Other Ideas For Advanced Level

Asides from using the Cricut to make projects for your home, there is the extra advantage of creating stuff to adorn yourself. These include your earrings, bracelets, necklaces, and other adornments.

**Earrings**

It is possible that you might have been interested in making earrings while using your Cricut but you do not have the technical know-how. Do not stress further, this part is going to give you a step by step breakdown of how to go about this.

*Materials and Tools needed:*

- Cricut Machine
- Cricut Blade (comes with the machine)
- Faux leather
- Metallic Vinyl
- Purple Standard Cutting Mat
- Transfer Tape
- Nose Pliers
- Spatula
- Earring Hooks
- Scissors
- Hole Punch
- Scraper or Cricut EasyPress

*The steps include:*

1. You should be logged on to your Design Space on your personal computer or iPad.
2. Once you are logged in to your Design Space, there is no limit to what design of earrings you can make. Create a new project and select the "Insert Image" option. You can then use the "Search" option to obtain any shape of your desire.
3. Once you have found your desired shape, you should then insert it. How your iron-on accents would look like depends on your decision.

4. You can then use the "Slice" and "Weld" options found in the Layer Panel to make different slice shapes for your earrings.
5. Upon completing your design, you should select the "Make It" option. It is also important to be certain that you have your second mat mirrored as your cutting material is iron-on. Your first mat should be the Faux Leather while the second should be the Metallic Iron-On.
6. Start with a piece of Cricut Metallic Leather and position it on a Strong Grip mat in a sweeping manner, apply pressure to have the leather stick to the mat. In the case when the mat and leather do not stick together, you should use masking tapes to hold firm the sides of the mat and leather together.
7. The start wheels should then be moved to the far-right side of the machine. The Fine-Point Blade should then be replaced with the Deep-Cut Blade. The Deep-Cut Blade is to ensure proper and full cutting of the material.
8. In your Design Space, click on "Make," and then have Faux Leather chosen as the material option for cutting.
9. Have the Mat placed into the Cricut machine and you should proceed to cut? When the cut is finished, remove the mat, and with the most care, you should then have the excess leather removed and this has the earrings left alone on the mat.

10. The star wheels should then be returned to the initial position from which they were moved while the blades should be switched back to Fine-Point Blade from the Deep-Cut Blade. For the earring that you have decided on, you should cut a sufficiently sizable portion of iron-on and then have it applied on the mat.
11. The Cricut weeding tools should then be engaged to weed the specific earrings by having the excess vinyl peeled back with great care. The earring should be covered with a sheet of transfer tape, and then the vinyl should also be burnished on the transfer tape. The hearing should then be cut into pairs as the white paper that backs them is removed. Leather earrings left on the purple mat will be perfectly lined up with the vinyl.
12. The vinyl should then be positioned on top of the earrings and then the vinyl is to be burnished on the leather. This can be done with the scraper or by heating up your Cricut EasyPress—the recommended settings for the EasyPress varies as the base material you are using determined the temperature you will be using.
13. You should then have the transfer tape peeled off so as to have your earrings uncovered. You should then live off the mat each earring with your Spatula.
14. You should then attach the metal hooks to your earrings. You should open your eyes in the earring using a pair of needle-nose pliers. This should be done gently and also the

hole should be wide enough for the hook to fit through. The hook should then be inserted in the earring through the hole you would have made at the back using the punch.

15. You should then close the hole with your nose pliers.

Now, your darling handmade earrings are set and ready to be used.

**Bracelets**

The bracelet is a project that is easy to create on your own. This project needs just a couple of materials and tools.

*Materials and tools needed:*

- Cricut Machine
- Leather Bracelet
- Cricut Iron-on
- EasyPress

- EasyPress Mat
- Weeding Tool
- LightGrip Cutting Mat
- Measuring Tape

*The steps include:*

1. Log on to your Design Space on your personal computer or iPad.
2. Once you are logged in, you can then proceed to have your SVG file downloaded. Once you have downloaded the SVG file, you should then upload it to your Design Space. Make sure you resize your design and make sure it is going to fit well on your leather bracelet.
3. You should then load your mat. Remember to have the shiny part of your Iron-on facing the mat. Your Cricut should then be set to the material "Iron-on" and then it is ready to cut.
4. Once the design has been cut-out, you should then proceed to weed with your weeding tool. You should do this with extreme care so as not to miss out on any material.
5. Your EasyPress should then be preheated to the necessary temperature. You should check online to find out what temperature the EasyPress is suitable for each material.
6. Have the weeded cut-out image positioned as you wish on the leather bracelet and then have both of them inserted in your EasyPress for about 30 seconds.

7. The transfer paper should then be peeled off.
8. This allows the unveiling of your cute handmade bracelet.

**Necklaces**

Necklaces are such wonderful items that can be giving out to friends, families, etc. The Cricut machine allows you the opportunity to have your own customized necklace with any material of your choice. Imagine getting to a store to purchase this nice necklace but it is not available in gold but leather. The disappointment you would feel. However, you can create your own necklace according to your taste.

*Materials and tools needed:*

- Cricut Machine
- Strong Grip Mat

- Transfer Tape
- Necklace (of any material of your choice)
- Jump Ring
- Pliers
- Glue

*The steps include:*

1. You should be logged in on your Design Space on your personal computer or iPads.
2. You can choose to download the SVG file of your choice or decide to create the design yourself.
3. You should then proceed to cut your image. You will have different options that are before you, however, you should select the option "Leather, Heavy" as this will be effective for your tooling leather.
4. There will be an on-screen instruction to guide you on how the different layers of your design can be cut.
5. The cardstock layers, Cardstock and Mod Podge should then be glued together. The safety pin should be used to make sure the glue is removed from tiny holes on each cut-out word.
6. The adhesive foil should then be applied, and to ensure it adheres well, it should be firmly pressed.
7. This should then be left to dry once the charm has been sealed.

8. You can then add jump rings through each hole in the charm to which the necklaces will be added. The jump rings are made by the jeweler pliers.
9. Your necklace is then ready for use.

# Chapter 11. Other Projects Using Cricut Design Space

**Night Sky Pillow**

*Supplies Needed:*

- Black, dark blue, or dark purple fabric
- Heat transfer vinyl in gold or silver
- Cutting mat
- Polyester batting
- Weeding tool or pick
- Cricut EasyPress

*Instructions:*

1. Decide the shape you want for your pillow, and cut two matching shapes out of the fabric.
2. Open Cricut Design Space and create a "New Project."
3. Select the "Image" button in the lower left-hand corner and search "Start."
4. Select the stars of your choice and click "Insert."
5. Place the iron-on material on the mat.
6. Send the design to the Cricut.
7. Use the weeding tool, or pick to remove excess material.
8. Remove the material from the mat.

9. Place the iron-on material on the fabric.
10. Use the EasyPress to adhere it to the iron-on material.
11. Sew the two fabric pieces together, leaving allowance for a seam and a small space open.
12. Fill the pillow with polyester batting through the small open space.
13. Sew the pillow shut.
14. Cuddle up to your starry pillow!

## Clutch Purse

*Supplies Needed:*

- Two fabrics, one for the exterior and one for the interior
- Fusible fleece
- Fabric cutting mat
- D-ring
- Sew-on snap
- Lace
- Zipper
- Sewing machine
- Fabric scissors
- Keychain or charm of your choice

*Instructions:*

1. Open Cricut Design Space and create a "New Project."

2. Select the "Image" button in the lower left-hand corner and search for "Essential Wallet."
3. Select the essential wallet template, and click "Insert."
4. Place the fabric on the mat.
5. Send the design to the Cricut.
6. Remove the fabric from the mat.
7. Attach the fusible fleecing to the wrong side of the exterior fabric.
8. Attach lace to the edges of the exterior fabric.
9. Assemble the D-ring strap.
10. Place the D-ring onto the strap and sew into place.
11. Fold the pocket pieces' wrong side out over the top of the zipper, and sew it into place.
12. Fold the pocket's wrong side in and sew the sides.
13. Sew the snap onto the pocket.
14. Lay the pocket on the right side of the main fabric lining so that the corners of the pocket's bottom are behind the curved edges of the lining fabric. Sew the lining piece to the zipper tape.
15. Fold the lining behind the pocket and iron in place.
16. Sew on the other side of the snap.
17. Trim the zipper so that it is not overhanging the edge.
18. Sew the two pocket layers to the exterior fabric across the bottom.
19. Sew around all of the layers.
20. Trim the edges with fabric scissors.

21. Turn the clutch almost completely inside out and sew the opening to close it.
22. Turn the clutch all the way inside out and press the corners into place.
23. Attach your charm or keychain to the zipper.
24. Carry your new clutch wherever you need it!

**Personalized Water Bottle**

*Supplies Needed:*

- A water bottle with a smooth surface (these are very easy to find in superstores)
- Transfer tape
- A brayer or a scraper
- Outdoor vinyl

*Instructions:*

1. Your first step is to open the design app. Let us say for this example that we are going to be making the name "Adam."
2. Choose a font that you like, and then use the eyeball icon in the Layers panel.
3. Create a second text box, and you can make the initial letter bigger.
4. Now, you will need to attach the two layers together so that the "Name" and the "Initial" are cut out together.
5. Resize and make it fit your water bottle.
6. To make sure that this will adhere to your bottle, you will need to use transfer tape. The brayer can help here because you can help press the transfer tape down.
7. Start in the center of the letter and work out when adhering to the bottle. Be sure to smooth all bubbles.
8. Peel off the tape very carefully, and then you are finished.

**Fabric Coaster**

*Supplies Needed:*

- The Maker
- Rotary cut and mat, or a pair of scissors
- A sewing machine
- An iron
- Cotton fabric and a coordinating thread
- Fusible fleece

*Instructions:*

1. Cut your fabric to the inches you need to fit on your cutting mat.
2. Open Design Space and hit the button that says "New Project."
3. Click on "Shapes" and then insert a heart shape. You will do this from the pop-up window.
4. Resize your heart to 5.5 inches. Click "Make It."
5. Change the project copies to four (left corner at the top). Then, click "Apply."
6. Click "Continue" (bottom right).
7. Set your material to medium fabrics like cotton.
8. Load your mat with the fabric attached; Cut.
9. Repeat all steps, but this time, you will place the fusible fleece on the cutting mat.
10. Change the heart shape to 5.7"
11. When you select the material, click "View More" and then type in "Fusible Fleece."
12. Cut out two fleece hearts.
13. Attach a fleece heart to the back of a fabric heart. You will use a hot iron to do this (be careful not to burn yourself).
14. Repeat with the second heart.
15. With the right sides together, sew two heart shapes together. Make sure the fleece is attached. Leave a gap in the stitches for turning.
16. Clip the curves.

17. Turn the heart's right side out, then press with the iron.
18. Fold in the edges of the opening and then press once more.
19. Stitch around the heart a quarter inch from the edge.

**Glitter Tumbler**

*Supplies Needed:*

- Painters tape
- Mod podge and paint brush
- Epoxy
- Glitter
- Stainless steel tumbler
- Spray paint
- Vinyl
- Sandpaper wet/dry
- Gloves
- Plastic cup
- Measuring cup
- Rubbing alcohol

*Instructions:*

1. Tape off the top and bottom of the tumbler.
2. Make sure to seal them well enough that paint will not get on either.

3. Spray paint twelve inches away from your tumbler in an area that is well ventilated.
4. Make sure that the items you used are approved and will not make you sick.
5. Once your tumbler is dry from the paint you have used you can add the glitter.
6. This will make a mess, so have something under it to catch the glitter.
7. Put the mod podge in a small container.
8. Use a flat paintbrush to put it on.
9. Take the lid off and rotate the cup adding glitter.
10. Make sure it is completely covered.
11. Make sure that an excess glitter will come off before removing the tape and letting it dry.
12. When dry take a flat brush that is clean, and stroke down the glitter to get any additional pieces not glued down.
13. Add a piece of tape above the glitter line.
14. Do the same to the bottom.
15. Get a plastic cup and gloves.
16. Use the epoxy and measure equal parts of solution A and B into measuring cups. If it is a small mug you only need about 5 ml each. Larger ones need 10 ml.
17. Pour them both in a cup and scrape down the sides using a wooden stick.
18. Stir for three minutes and pop all bubbles.
19. Your gloves should be on but if not, put them on now.

20. Add the glitter to the epoxy and stir.
21. Add the mixture to the tumbler and turn it often while you are doing this. Having a roller or something to turn it on will help and make sure it is in the air so nothing is touching it.
22. When the drugs are not coming as fast, you can slow the turning down but while it is the turning is constant.
23. Take the tape off after forty-five minutes.
24. Spin the tumbler for five hours and it should be dry, if not leave it on a foam roller overnight.
25. Sand the tumbler gently with wet sandpaper.
26. When it is all smooth from sanding clean it with rubbing alcohol.
27. Then open the Cricut design space and cut out your glitter vinyl.
28. Weed the design.
29. Add strong grip transfer tape.
30. Transfer the decal to the tumbler.

This is a very hard project that takes a lot of time and you need to make sure that children are nowhere near these products, as it will be fatal to them if they swallow them. Another thing to remember is spinning and making sure it is dry. By following these instructions, you should have a great glitter tumbler that you can take anywhere and rock a stylish look. This is a great idea for business owners as well because decorated tumblers are a hot commodity right now and everyone loves them.

# Personalized Mermaid Bottle

*Supplies Needed:*

- You will need a water bottle with a smooth surface (these are very easy to find in dollar stores, superstores, specialty stores, or really any store you would like to go to)
- Transfer tape
- A brayer or a scraper
- Outdoor vinyl

*Instructions:*

1. Your first step is to open the design app. Let us say, for this example, we are going to be making a mermaid.
2. Choose a font that you like and then use the eyeball icon in the Layers panel. If you do not want to make it yourself, simply go into the design space and choose one of their ready to make projects.
3. Create a second text box, and you can make the picture bigger.
4. Now you will need to attach the two layers together so that the picture and the initials, cut together.
5. Resize and make it fit your water bottle.
6. To make sure that this will adhere to your bottle you will need to use transfer tape. The brayer can help here because you can help press the transfer tape down.

7. Start in the center of the letter and work out when adhering to the bottle. Be sure to smooth all bubbles.
8. Peel off the tape very carefully, and then you are finished
9. To make the shark, follow the same instructions.

By utilizing the tips in this book, you will be able to make some great projects and really get used to your machine and its inner workings, as well as unleash your own creativity and learn. The Cricut machines have made crafting so much easier and a lot more fun. The fact that Cricut also works with companies for you to be able to use their designs if you want to utilize them, makes this perfect for fans of pop culture.

Enjoy taking your crafting skills to the next level and learning great new projects with the Cricut machines!

# Chapter 12. Other Projects Using Cricut Design Space (Part 2)

**Wedding Table Plan**

*To make your plant wedding table plan, you will need:*

- Cricut Machine
- 1 box of 25 Pollen sheets 210x297 mm
- 210g Ivory
- Extra strong double-sided adhesive tape—6mm x 10m
- High-temperature glue gun
- White metal ring 25 cm
- Straight scissors 17 cm
- 1 natural kraft string

*Discover all the steps below:*

STEP 1/13—Using the Cricut, cut multiple sheets using the different shades of green card stock.

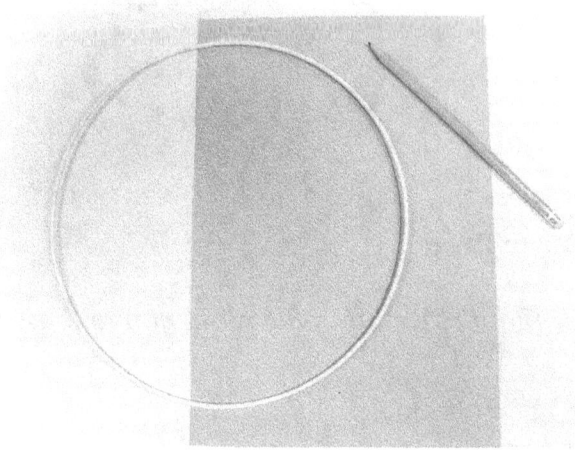

STEP 2/13—Trace the inner and outer outline of the half of the ring on green card stock with a pencil, and cut out the half-moon, leaving enough room on both sides to be able to fold it around the ring.

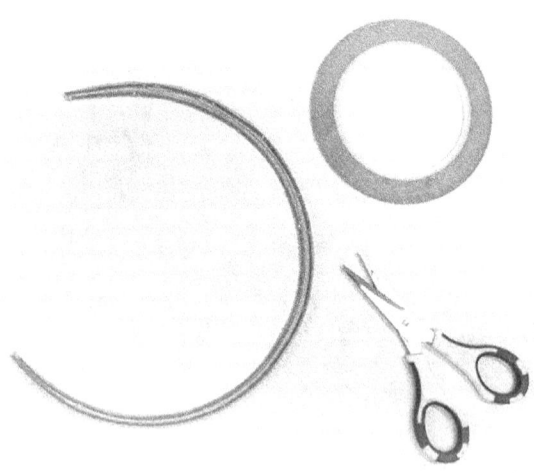

STEP 3/13—Stick the double-sided adhesive tape on the half-moon.

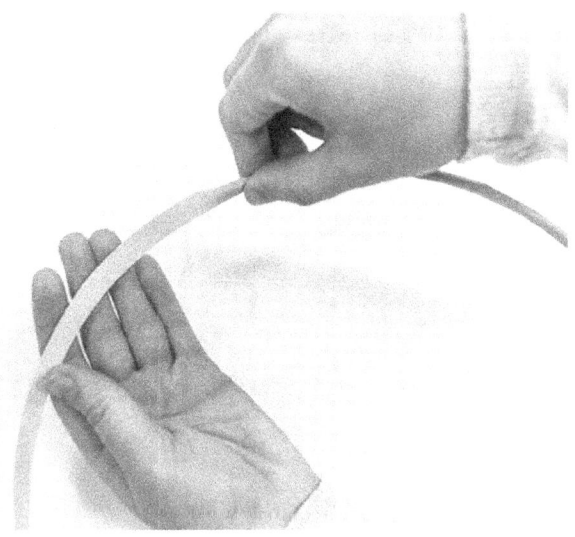

STEP 4/13—Fold it around half of the hoop, pinching the edges so that they are secure. This edge will serve as a base for easily gluing your paper sheets.

STEP 5/13—Arrange the different cut sheets on the part of the ring covered with paper and glue the elements with a glue gun.

STEP 6/13—Using the Cricut and the Natural Leaves dye, cut the berries out of the cream card stock.

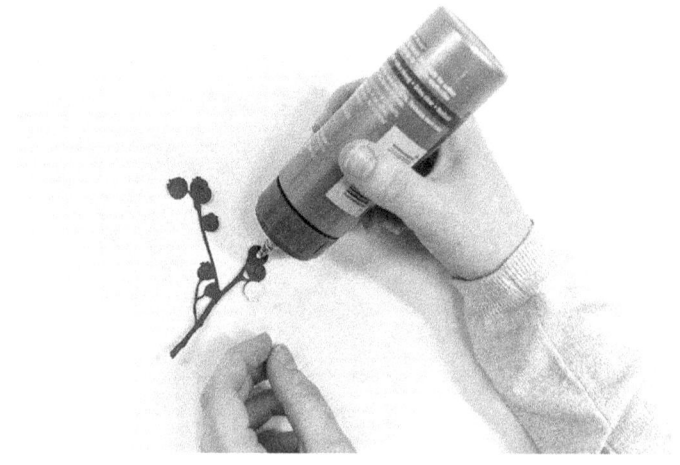

STEP 7/13—Glue the berries on the corresponding branches of the set to bring out the berries.

STEP 8/13—Insert and glue the berry branches among the other leaves where you want to add shades of color.

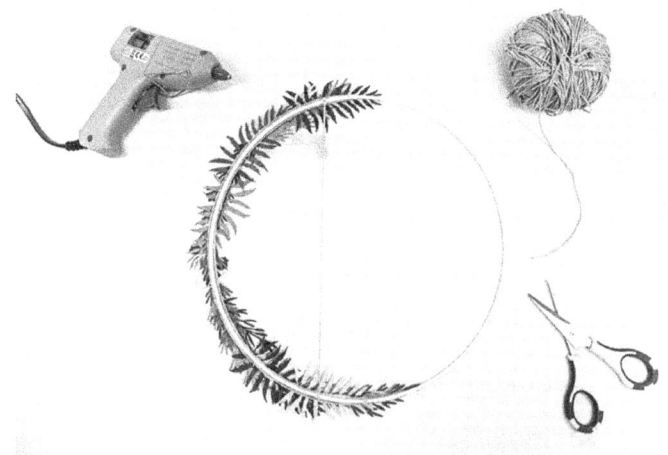

STEP 9/13—Tie the string to the back of the metal ring with the glue gun, cut off the excess if necessary

STEP 10/13—Print the table numbers on the cream card stock, cut out in a circle and glue it on the string, towards the center of the ring.

STEP 11/13—Print the names of the guests on the cream paper and cut them out with scissors, forming banners.

STEP 12/13—Create your seating plan and paste the guest names wherever you want!

STEP 13/13—Create as many rings as there are guest tables for your wedding and arrange them on a recovered wooden pallet.

## Paper Decoration

*To make this tropical decoration, you will need:*

- Cricut
- Set of 6 Scrapbooking paper sheets
- Leaf—30.5x30.5cm—petrol blue.
- Leaf —30.5x30.5cm—menthol green
- Leaf—30.5x30.5cm—lime green
- Leaf—30.5x30.5cm—spring green
- Slate scrapbooking sheet—30x30cm
- Sheet of 34 epoxy stickers
- 8 card stock polaroid frames
- Assortment of 40 die-cuts
- 100m two-tone spool - Sky blue
- 16 mini clothespins 35 mm
- Vivaldi smooth sheet A4
- 240g—Canson—white n ° 1
- Precision cutter and 3 blades
- Blue cutting mat—2mm—A3
- Acrylic and aluminum ruler 30cm black
- Precision scissors 13.5cm blue bi-material rings
- 3D adhesive squares
- Mahé Tools—scrapbooking
- Pack of 6 HB graphite pencils

*Preparation time:* 2h

*Techniques:* Stencil, Collage, Origami, Folding, Tropical

*Discover below all the steps to realize your summer decoration "Tropical Paradise":*

1. Gather the materials.

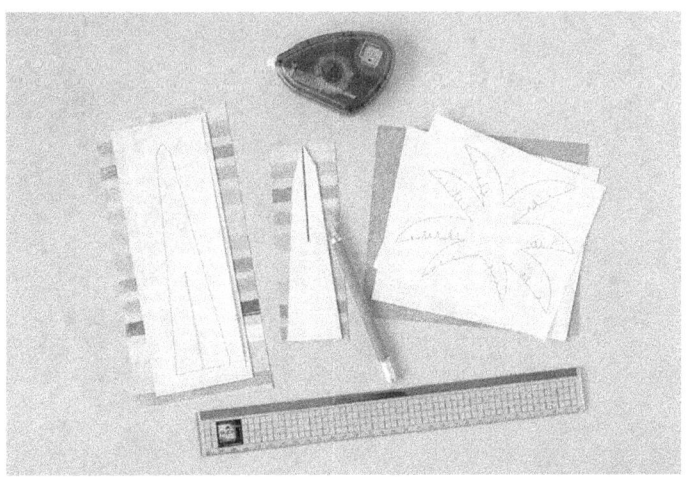

2. Using the template and a pencil, reproduce the palm tree on the papers in the collection.

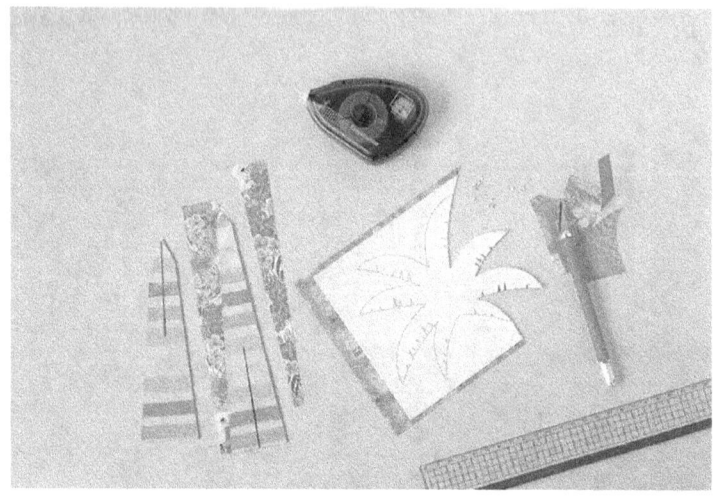

3. Cut out using Cricut.

4. Assemble the trunk of the palm tree. Glue the foliage. Using the template, reproduce the traces of the cocktail support on thin cardboard, following the dimensions indicated. Cover it with the collection paper.

5. After having cut in the slate sheet: 1 x (8.5 x 8.5 cm). Choose a Polaroid. Glue the slate sheet to the back of the Polaroid. Using a chalk pen, write "Cocktail of the day." Decorate with the stickers. Fold the support at the dotted lines.

6. Using the templates and a pencil, draw the leaves and flowers on the paper and on the collection paper. Draw.

7. Choose photos. Cut them to size: 8.5 x 8.5 cm. Stick to the back of the Polaroids.

8. Glue the leaves and flowers together. Cut the string to the desired dimensions and glue it to the back of the flowers. Glue the birds on the string and hang the photos using mini clips.

And here is a pretty summer and tropical decoration! Beautiful evenings in perspective!

## Crepe Paper Flowers

*Completion time:* more than 2 hours

*Difficulty:* 1/3

*To make this bouquet of crepe paper flowers, you will need:*

- Assortment of 10 rolls of crepe paper, or discover our range of crepe papers
- 20 thread stems with flower 1mm x 50 cm
- Vinyl glue
- 4 pairs of multi-use scissors
- Cutout template to download, print, and cut.

*Find all the detailed steps below:*

1. Creation of yellow flowers:

Print the template and cut it out on Cricut. Cut 5 petals out of yellow florist crepe paper. Be sure to place the vertical template in the direction of the grooves of the crepe paper. Cut a 2.5 x 5 cm strip of orange florist crepe paper. Bisect a binding wire with a clamp cutting.

Stretch each petal by placing your thumbs in the middle of the petals. Dig with your thumbs apart. The petals become very rounded. Finely notch the orange strip. Paste up the binding wire and winding the paper to form the pistils.

Stick the pistils in the hollow of a first petal. Glue the second petal slightly offset by about 3mm. Glue all the petals until they half cover the first petal. Pinch the basis for refining.

Cut a strip of green crepe paper about 0.5 x 15 cm long. Shoot it. Glue one end to the base of the petals. Apply glue and wrap it tightly around the rod. Leave to dry. Prepare 10 yellow flowers like this.

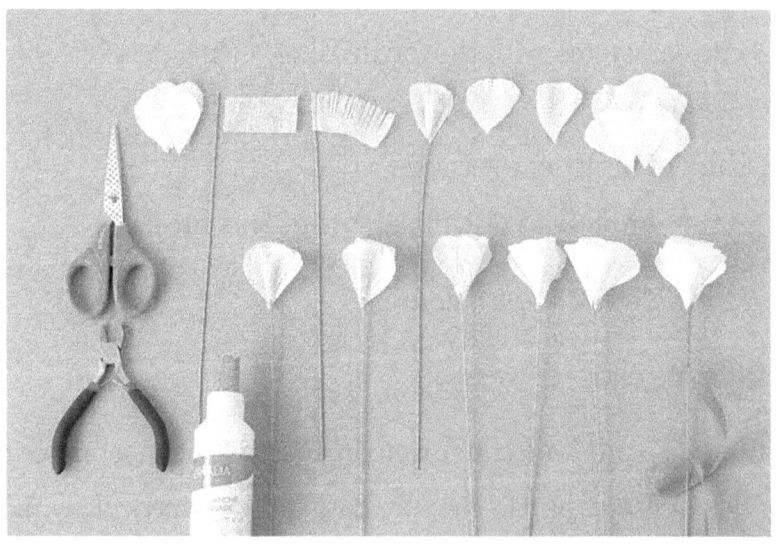

2. Creation of white:

Cut 10 petals out of white florist crepe paper. Be sure to place the vertical template in the direction of the grooves of the crepe paper. Cut a 2.5 x 5 cm strip of yellow florist crepe paper. Cut a wire to be tied in half using wire cutters.

Pinch the top edge of a petal starting from the left and spacing the inches 2 millimeters apart. Stretch the paper. Move your thumbs and repeat the operation every 5 millimeters, to form little ruffles. Do the same for each petal. Place thumbs in the middle of the petals. Dig lightly with your thumbs apart without completely stretching the paper. Finely notch the yellow strip. Stick the top of the binding wire and winding the paper to form the pistils.

Stick the pistils in the hollow of a first petal. Glue the second petal offset by about 5 millimeters. Glue all the petals by rolling the petals to surround the flower several times. Pinch the base to refine it.

Cut a strip of green crepe paper about 0.5 x 15 cm long. Shoot it. Glue one end to the base of the petals. Apply glue and wrap it tightly around the rod. Let dry. Prepare and 10 white flowers.

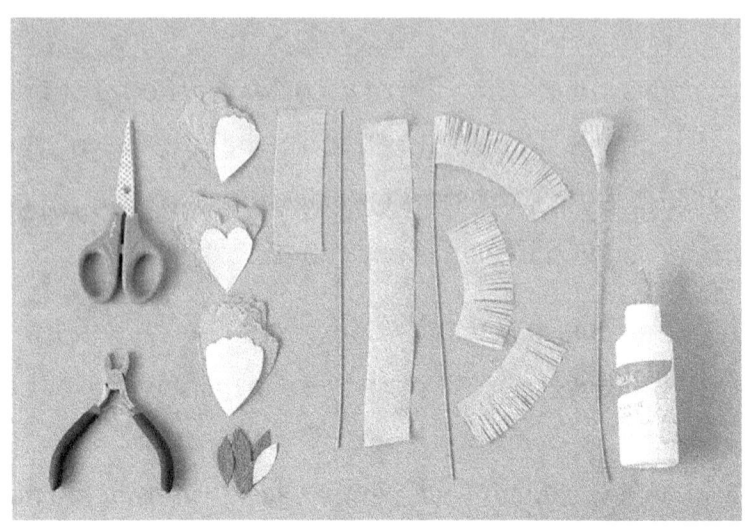

3. Creating peony flowers:

Cut 7 petals of the first template out of bright pink florist crepe paper. Prepare 7 heart-shaped petals and 6 large petals and 5 sepals in green crepe paper. Make sure to place the template vertically in the direction of the paper grooves crepe.

Cut a 3.5 x 11 cm strip of orange florist crepe paper. Cut into both a binding wire with a clamp cutting.

Stretch the orange strip. Fold it in 3 and cut. Finely notch each orange strip. Glue the first strip to the top of the wire to be bound and roll up the paper to form the pistils. Add the second, then the third strip. Spread the pistils to give them volume. Pinch the base to refine it.

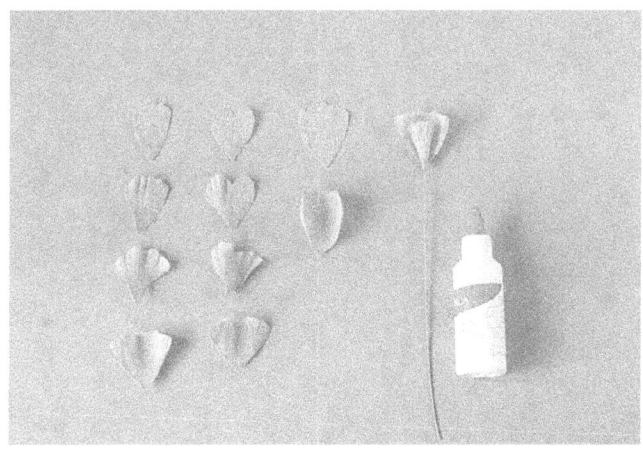

4. Give the form to the petals:

Take the first set of petals. Pinch the top edge of a petal starting from the left and spacing the inches 2 millimeters apart. Stretch the paper. Move your thumbs and repeat the operation every 5 millimeters, to form little ruffles. Do the same for each petal. Place thumbs in the middle of the petals. Widen slightly, keeping an inch without fully extend the paper.

Prepare the same way the petals in a heart shape.

For larger petals, stretch them one by one. Place thumbs in the middle of the petals. Dig with your thumbs apart. The petals become very rounded.

Stick the pistils in the hollow of a first petal.

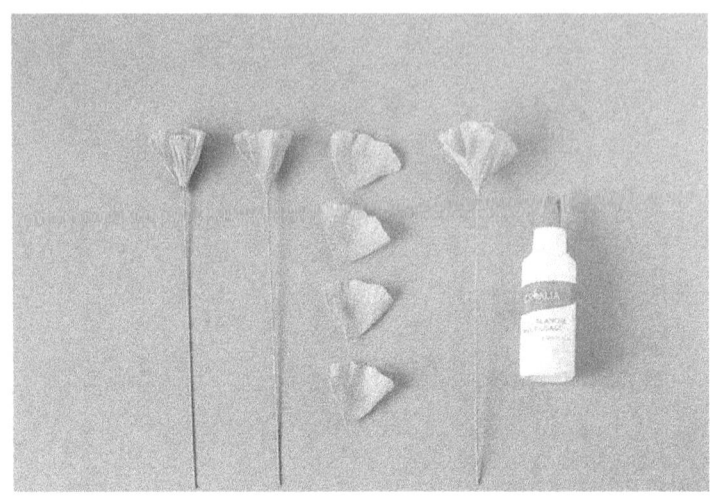

Step 5.

Glue the second petal offset by about 5 millimeters. Glue by wrapping the first 7 petals to surround the flower several times. Pinch the base to refine it.

Step 6:

Glue the second set of heart-shaped petals onto the flower. Glue each petal a little higher than the base, on the first petals to create a more garnished effect. Paste wrapping around the petals of the flower.

Finish by gluing the last set of 6 rounded petals, arranging to surround the flower only once.

Step 7.

Turn the flower over and glue the sepals starting from the stem to cover the base of the flower. Cut a strip of green crepe paper about 0.4 x 15 cm long. Shoot it. Glue it to the base of the sepals. Apply glue and wrap it tightly around the rod. Let dry. Prepare 5 hot pink peonies and 4 soft pink peonies in this way.

Step 8. The foliage.

Print the template and cut it out using Cricut. Cut 10 leaves from green florist crepe paper. Be sure to place the vertical template in the direction of the grooves of the crepe paper. Cut a wire to be tied in half using wire cutters. Paste the wire bonding at the center of the foliage. Cut a strip of green crepe paper about 0.4 x 15 cm long. Shoot it. The paste to the base of the foliage. Apply glue and wrap it tightly around the rod. Let dry. Prepare 10 green leaves in this way.

## Floral Letter in Watercolor

*Time:* 60 minutes.

*To make your floral letter in watercolor, you will need:*

- Cricut Maker
- Box of 12 Aqua pencils
- 3 watercolor brushes
- Watercolor pad 25 x 25 cm
- 200 Double-sided adhesive foam squares—Cerealia
- Extra strong double-sided adhesive tape—6mm x 10m—Cerealia
- Template to download and print.

*Find all the steps:*

STEP 1/9—Print the templates and using the tracing paper, reproduce the letter chosen on the watercolor paper as well as the flowers.

STEP 2/9—Color the letter with watercolor pencils. Make areas darker to create contrast.

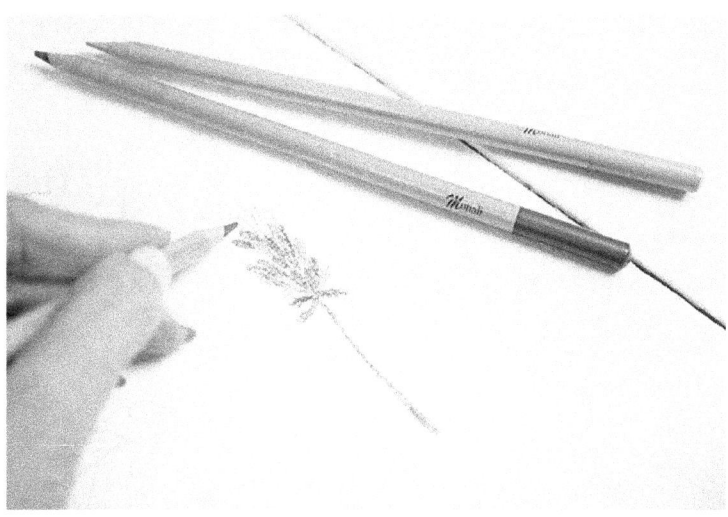

STEP 3/9—Apply water to the entire letter with a watercolor brush.

STEP 4/9—Color the plants. For flowers, put different colors on the petals.

STEP 5/9—With the watercolor brush, apply water and blend the colors together.

STEP 6/9—For the foliage, apply the first color and add lines of different colors to create nuances.

STEP 7/9—Cut out the patterns using a Cricut maker.

STEP 8/9—Glue the patterns on the letter using the foam squares. Then glue everything on the canvas with double-sided tape.

STEP 9/9—Your floral monogram is ready.

# Conclusion

Thank you for making it to the end! More and more people choose to create their own materials, invitations, and holiday cards for scrapbooking. These options allow more personalization than their off-the-shelf substitutes. Not only are the home-made invitations more customized, but they are also much less expensive than stores. Cricut personal cutting machines make it possible to create a professional craft project anytime even for those with little time and even less experience.

Cricut cutting machines are locally available in craft shops and some department stores with art and craft sections. But the best deals are usually found online. The entry-level type with willingly obtainable sales prices of about 100 dollars is more than adequate for the occasional do-it-yourselfer. It can produce thousands of diverse shape groupings and needs little maintenance. More experienced craftsmen, or those managing home enterprises that create personalized paper products, may find that larger models meet their needs.

These machines are mechanized and much easier than older manual cutters to use. They can cut even heavy paper inventories, in most cases, enabling scrapbookers to create designs with a range of colors and textures. A number of sites offer advice from regular amateur users to provide guidance on how to use a new machine. They can be a valuable source of information and inspiration to illustrate the best use of the machine. While these sites are a great destination, the best feature of a Cricut home machine is the ability to create completely one-of-a-kind websites. Experiment with new shapes and color combinations to create something unique and memorable.

Cricut cutting machines are sufficiently versatile for any type of craft project. Make skilled-looking scrapbooks with personal Cricut cutting machines.

For any scrapbooker, a Cricut cutting machine is a must-have. These devices allow users to decouple paper into various interesting types, making it simple, and fun to personalize every page in a scrapbook. Designed to be small enough to take you on your journey, they will take up little space at home and can be brought with you at any scrapbooking party you attend. They are the perfect tool for anyone who wants a user-friendly way to create unique borders, inserts, and other decorating pages.

Cricut machines can produce shapes from 1" to more than 5" high anywhere. Simple to adjust metal cutting patterns, most styles of craft paper produce standardized shapes. These forms can be used to add custom letters, cheerful shapes, or thought-provoking borders that represent any page's content. While many different card stock thicknesses may be used, scrapbookers should know that paper in a heavier grade might make the blades dull faster.

This means that the sharpness of the blade should always be checked and replaced if appropriate in order to ensure good performance.

A Cricut computer is not a small investment. Prices start at about $100 and some people cannot use this cutting machine. When considering, however, the costs of the production of pre-cut letters and forms, the computer will ultimately pay for itself, as are noticed by most committed enthusiasts. These may also be used for other documents, such as individual invites, gift tags, and holiday cards.

www.ingramcontent.com/pod-product-compliance
Lightning Source LLC
Chambersburg PA
CBHW071516080526
44588CB00011B/1446